Perseverance

the

seven skills

you need to

survive, thrive, and

accomplish more than

you ever imagined

Tim Hague

VIKING

VIKING

an imprint of Penguin Canada, a division of Penguin Random House Canada Limited

Canada • USA • UK • Ireland • Australia • New Zealand • India • South Africa • China

First published 2018

www.penguinrandomhouse.ca

LIBRARY AND ARCHIVES CANADA CATALOGUING IN PUBLICATION

    Hague, Tim, author
Perseverance : the seven skills you need to survive, thrive, and accomplish more than you ever imagined / Tim Hague.

Issued in print and electronic formats.
ISBN 978-0-7352-3366-9 (hardcover).—ISBN 978-0-7352-3367-6 (HTML)

    1. Hague, Tim. 2. Hague, Tim—Health. 3. Parkinson's disease—Patients—Canada—Biography. 4. Determination (Personality trait). 5. Perseverance (Ethics). 6. Conduct of life. I. Title.

RC382.H33 2018   362.1968'330092   C2017-907150-5
                                             C2017-907151-3

Cover and interior design by Leah Springate
Cover images: (ant) designer_an; (leaf) jirateep sankote, both Shutterstock.com

Printed and bound in the United States of America

10 9 8 7 6 5 4 3 2 1

Penguin
Random House
VIKING CANADA

To Eleanor, Mom, and Dad
Thank you for this life

Contents

per·se·ver·ance: To carry on in your course of action, even in the face of difficulty, with little or no evidence of success.

Introduction

WE ALL HAVE AN IDEA of what perseverance means, but it was only relatively late in life that I really came to understand it.

Our North American culture often tells us that we should look, feel, and be successful. Yet any success I've had has come only after significant ordeals, and rarely did I ever feel successful along the way. But I've learned to persevere. This is an important point to hold on to: perseverance can be learned. We can grow in our ability to withstand difficult times. We can learn to push forward in the face of failure. We can develop the determination to keep slogging ahead until we reach that remarkable day when someone in our life points out how "lucky" we've been.

It's funny how so many of those who work hard and simply stay in the game get "lucky." Without a doubt, many successful people will tell you that they've experienced lots of luck in their journey. That's because they stayed on the journey. They never quit. They learned to persevere.

I've been forced, specifically by Parkinson's disease, to learn simplicity within perseverance. I've come to see that I can't do it all, that at times I do need a hand, and that I certainly can't control every outcome in life. Although that sounds like a lot of things I can't do, I've learned that I can pay better attention, focus carefully, and end up accomplishing more. And as I find that there are things I can control, my character is deepened and I discover contentment.

Perseverance—a great big long word that's often attached to difficulties. Yet if we learn its lessons our lives will be deeper, richer, and more vibrant than we ever imagined.

Jenna was ten when her father was diagnosed with Parkinson's at the age of fifty. Unlike most ten-year-olds, she understood the gravity of the diagnosis—and set herself to doing something about this thing that had attacked her dad. When she learned that funds were needed to help people live well with the disease and to spur on research for a cure, she decided to help those who could help her dad. Five years later, "Jenna's Toonies for Tulips" campaign is going strong; she's raised more than $50,000 for Parkinson's. (In Canada, a toonie is the two-dollar coin.)

Jenna is the daughter of a good friend of mine. I'm continually amazed and inspired by her work for Parkinson's; she's a constant reminder of the simplicity of what it is I want to do with my life. Like Jenna, I want to help. Whether it's her dad or others like him, I want to see people lifted above the misery of their circumstances and inspired to live their best.

Hence this book. My greatest desire in writing it is to shine a light deep into people's souls and convince them that there is a better way. Throughout the book I'll provide practical steps, but my first goal is to help us see the bright reality of what can be. Then we can set ourselves on the course to that reality.

Later I'll discuss how this journey is best traveled with others. I've learned that I can't make it on my own; instead, I've experienced the best of life in community. The most important members of mine are my family. At the age of fifty-two I'm a husband of thirty-two years to my lovely wife, Sheryl. We have four incredible children (two boys, two girls), a beautiful daughter-in-law, and one of God's greatest gifts to humankind, a granddaughter.

By profession, I am a nurse. I reside in that unique minority of males who make up roughly five percent of the profession. This is my chosen career, or at least the one I backed into. By passion, I am a writer, speaker, founder of a charity, entrepreneur, runner, and follower of Christ. These are the many important adjectives that describe who I am. Not listed in any particular order.

Then there's that pesky little friend named Parkinson's, which came into my life at a comparatively early age and which allows me to call myself patient, client, advocate, and fighter. I have a complex relationship with this "friend." I love much of what Parkinson's has brought me, while hating it and specifically its symptoms. It's a disease that typically afflicts individuals over the age of sixty. Seldom is it a bother to those under fifty, with only about ten percent of the Parkinson's population diagnosed before the mid-century mark. I was forty-six.

Parkinson's is a progressive nerve disease of the brain that in time leads to a debilitation of a person's motor functions. In other words, you can no longer control the movements of your body. The individual with Parkinson's loses the important ability to produce a chemical called dopamine, leading to the classic symptoms of tremor, stiffness, slowness, and loss of balance. Along with myriad lesser-known evils referred to as "non-motor symptoms."

Not all lottery wins are good things, and I'm not particularly happy about having won this one. But although my new best friend—whom I hate—has brought a certain level of grief into my life, it also played a direct role in my next lottery win.

At Sheryl's urging, my son Tim Jr. and I applied to appear on *The Amazing Race Canada*. We had little expectation of hearing back. But Sheryl was certain we'd get an interview; they'll be intrigued, she said, by my Parkinson's diagnosis. Naturally, she was right.

Running that race has changed everything. It's not only taught me valuable lessons in how to persevere but also allowed me the opportunity to pursue my passions.

Winning was incredible, of course. The trips, the prizes, the cash—it was all more exciting than words can describe. Yet my passions have never had much to do with things. As a nurse, it was always my desire to care for individuals. Early on, as a youth pastor, I wanted to help students find their way in life. Since then Sheryl and I have been involved with a number of charities and community organizations, and the race has given us the chance to pursue these activities with renewed vigor. It, and Parkinson's, have led to many exciting adventures that I wouldn't have otherwise thought possible, from the founding of our charity, U-Turn Parkinson's, to the development of a speaking career that has taken me around the globe.

So in writing this book, I want to inspire you to view life through a new lens—to see the potentially negative as an opportunity to grow. Running the race was an adventure, but what I want to share are the challenges of running it with Parkinson's and the lessons that taught me. To help you discover the joy that comes in persevering through hard times. I hope to encourage those who face this disease, to give them and their families the courage and strength to walk this very difficult path. But I also want to encourage those living with other hardships, whatever they may be. After all, the lessons on perseverance are universal, and can help the cancer patient and the corporate CEO alike.

Running the race with my eldest son was a wonderful experience. Many have asked about this aspect of the journey, and my answer is always the same: Tim Jr. made the perfect partner. He was fun and lighthearted, but also attentive to the needs of a father with Parkinson's. He was patient with my weaknesses and carried us when needed with the strength that comes only from a strapping young man. I'm so proud to have had the chance to create these memories with my son. I can't imagine having won this race without him.

It is my hope that you'll be inspired by our story—and that, like my friend Jenna, you'll grow in your ability to persevere. I hope it will give you what you need to run your race and win.

chapter 1

Beating
the
Odds

THE FIRST FEW MINUTES of our ferry ride across Toronto's Inner Harbour to Centre Island were surreal. Almost everywhere we went during the race we'd drawn crowds, or at least curious stares, as our camera and sound crews chased us about. But here on the ferry the cameras had been lowered. Our fellow passengers all but ignored us. For a few brief moments we were left to our own thoughts about what might shortly come to pass.

About halfway across the harbor, our brains switched from reflective "what ifs" back into race mode. We had to find Jon Montgomery, the host of *The Amazing Race Canada*, who'd be standing on the mat that marked the finish line. So as we drew ever closer to the shoreline we began scanning the trees, looking for any telltale signs of where that final destination might be. Every few minutes we'd catch a glimpse of some bit of moviemaking that would send our hearts racing, only to be disappointed. Once ashore, after two or three false sightings, we spotted Jon near the water's edge, perfectly framed in front of the CN Tower.

We stood up. Then we reviewed, as best as we could, the layout of the map we'd seen in the ferry terminal. Tim Jr. and I agreed that, once we got off the boat, we'd need to swing around a small portion of the island, cross a little bridge, and then head for the water's edge. That seemed straightforward enough. We were full of hope.

After flying over twenty-three thousand kilometers and visiting seven Canadian provinces and three territories, we were the first of nine teams to arrive at the final mat. Thus we took home the grand prize—two 2014 Chevrolet Corvettes, ten trips for two anywhere in the world where Air Canada flies, and a quarter million dollars—and *The Amazing Race Canada* winning title.

All because of Parkinson's. Had I not come down with it, the chances of us standing there would have been minute. That reality is troubling, creating no small amount of angst within me, and yet I am incredibly grateful. I'm thrilled to have been given the gift of running this race.

Finding the right words to describe our feelings in that moment is difficult. We'd come from behind so many times after having barely held on. Few if any had imagined we'd be in this position. And although we never doubted we could win, we never really thought we would. The moment was filled with a dumbstruck "We did it" and a crazy kind of happiness.

The lesson I came away with is the power of perseverance.

The race has taught me to take the long view, to push aside the negative emotions, to remember that the sun will come up tomorrow and you'll have another chance . . . if you only stay in the race. It has taught me to not step off the course, to not take my eye off the prize. There will be opportunity for redemption. Persevere.

In an intriguing twist of irony, it would seem that I've been learning and living this all my life.

chapter 2

A
False
Start

IN 1964 A BABY BOY was born into circumstances much different from most. The baby wasn't born into a home with a mom and a dad. As a matter of fact, the baby had no home. He was brought into the world in a small hospital on the Gulf of Mexico surrounded by the searing sands of Texas. Right away the baby was placed in an orphanage with the hope that one day he'd be adopted. There was no home, only a bed. There were no parents, only workers.

The mother was a twenty-year-old white girl from Iowa, in Middle America. The father was a thirtysomething-year-old married black man with children. In Iowa, in 1964, this was not going to work.

She came from a Christian family, and so abortion wasn't an option. Neither was keeping the baby. She was packed up and sent to a home in Texas for pregnant young women. The scandal was held close; few ever learned why the young lady had been gone.

In 1964, America was in turmoil. John Glenn became the first American astronaut to circle the globe; the Beatles hit number one on the American charts; Muhammad Ali became boxing's heavyweight champion of the world. The Vietnam War was raging; Walt Disney's *Mary Poppins* was a hit in theaters; and President Lyndon B. Johnson signed the Civil Rights Act into law, abolishing racial segregation in the United States. For those too young to remember what segregation was, it meant that white kids went to different schools from black kids and blacks did not eat in the same restaurants as whites. Race riots tore at America while Martin Luther King Jr. received the Nobel Peace Prize.

It was during this time that I was born a half-breed into a very black and white world.

What does one do with a "biracial" (as we were called) baby in 1964? You put up a "Free to Good Home" ad and see if you get any takers. But the reality was that there wasn't much of a market, and this particular product didn't have much of a shelf life. Let it get too old, and you'd be stuck with it for good.

So, with no immediate takers, I was put on the speaking circuit from birth. In an attempt to avoid having to raise me in an orphanage, I was taken from church to church, put on display, and offered to anyone who was willing. I'm told that it wasn't quite as dramatic as it seems, and that in fact it didn't take long until my parents and I found each other.

The head of the orphanage was speaking at a number of churches in the Kansas City area, and one evening, my parents attended. Mom, having seen the gorgeous (her word, not mine) baby boy, had to check into this a little more closely.

Mom and dad fell in love with not just me but also the thought of saving me from certain disaster.

In our present age, when adoptions can run to tens of thousands of dollars, it may come as a shock to hear that I cost them nothing and that the legal process basically boiled down to "Yeah, we'll take him." They saw a judge, signed some papers, and I had parents. I'm quite sure that, had they been astute enough to ask, they could have made a buck on the transaction.

As things turned out, they got a great deal on their first son, the orphanage had one less mouth to feed, and, well, I got a home with incredible parents. That last part will never cease to amaze me. When you consider the reality of the day, the odds against me, and the chances of my ending up as a drug-addled convict long since dead, I remain amazed that I'm here at all.

I ultimately learned that this had been a precarious time for me. There was simply no precedent for dealing with these kinds of children. With few interested in adopting mixed-race kids, the orphanage was at a loss as to what to do. At one point the decision was made to just keep me in the orphanage and raise me there. It turns out I owe my eventual adoption to my birth mom, who, upon learning of this plan, threw a fit. As she explained to me in later years, she threatened to take me home with her if a family wasn't found. How this "threat" motivated anyone is beyond me, but it did move them to at least try to find me a home. It would seem that either the orphanage or her parents weren't keen to have me back in Iowa, so a push was made on the adoption front.

With a successful adoption in place, my birth mom went home to Iowa. Only a very few were any the wiser to the tragedy that had engulfed her life. Meanwhile, I made my first move northward, to the state of Kansas, with my new mom and dad.

And so, growing up, this is who I was: a brown kid born with no home but chosen by someone else to be their son. Those someones went on to choose five more just like me in addition to the three children of their own. That makes a total of nine children, five boys and four girls. And given the significant age difference, our family essentially grew up in two sections. There were "the girls," my three older sisters, who were effectively out of the house by the time I came along. Then there were the six of us who were adopted. I've always marveled at that, but I'm so very grateful. We were a house of mutts, if you will, but we were all mutts together. We knew we'd been born of different lineages but had been joined in this family, and as such we were, and are, family. It was an extraordinarily different "normal," but it was our normal.

Our normal was that of a bunch of mixed-race children with white parents in a racially divided world. Standing out in a crowd was the norm. We rarely went to a restaurant, but what a spectacle we provided when we did. White mom and dad marching six brown kids to the largest table in the house. Heads would pivot, jaws would drop, the occasional scowl would be noted. We were not always welcome.

One of my favorite outings as a kid was to Zarda Dairy, the local ice cream shop. Again, this didn't happen often, but it was so sweet when it did. Dad would always get the same thing, a banana split with all the toppings. We kids would get our cones and revel in the special moment. I remember how happy these events would make Dad as he thrilled at the joy he knew it gave us. Not to mention the banana split or the fact that he'd been able to talk a few dollars out of the one who held the purse strings: Mom.

Having a brood of kids like this necessarily meant that there wasn't a lot of cash. In my early years, Dad was a pastor at small churches and worked as a janitor in schools on the side while Mom was a caregiver for elderly people. Each had come off the farm with a grade eight education. Our growing-up years were often extremely tight financially, but we were never poor in love.

Then there was school. I hated school. I remember heading off to kindergarten with new clothes and a new lunch pail, all excited. There I met Mrs. Popovich (along with "Soundy," her paper-bag puppet who taught us how to spell) and encountered more rules than a five-year-old could imagine. I clearly recall thinking after a couple of days, "Okay, that was fun. Time for something new." Sitting at a desk all day and doing this school stuff was just not working for me. There had to be more interesting things to do with one's day. But there was something else going on as well. The first seeds of realization were being planted: these other kids were not like me. Thus began what felt like an extremely long educational career that I never grew to like and longed to be free of.

I imagine that my middle-school experience was much like that of many others—a nightmare. It was in grades five and six that I fully came to understand my differentness. I began to realize that my world was made up of white people, black people, Latinos, and me. Now, when I say "me" I really mean "us," as in me and my adopted siblings. At the time we were an entity unto ourselves. Outside of my immediate family, I knew absolutely no other mixed-race individual.

It became apparent early on that it mattered to people what category I fit into. Virtually as far back as I can remember I'd be asked "What are you?" In the early years I'd say "white" because, of course, my parents were white. But it didn't take long for that error in thinking to be slammed to the ground. The first few times I was called a nigger I had no idea what it meant and finally had to ask Mom. I don't recall the explanation she gave, but it did become clear in my mind that many did not consider me "white."

The words we use to slander one another are ridiculous. Just as I was learning the N-word from a predominantly white group I was also learning the word "honky" from a predominantly black one. It turned out both groups had a term to set me apart as not belonging. And when someone spoke to me in Spanish, as they often did, it would be obvious when I replied that I didn't fit in that group either. In short, I simply did not fit.

However, I did fit at home, and this was my saving grace. As time went on and with the love and support of my parents I learned to manage my way in the world. As I got older I came to have many friends of all races who would bridge those differences. But that was later.

And as if fitting in and making friends weren't hard enough, I also had to figure out what color my girlfriend should be. You see, I was always too black for the white girl's dad, too white for the black girl's dad, and the wrong shade of brown for the Latino girl's dad. I'll never forget the father who suggested that I date "my own kind." At the time all I could think was "Who is that?" My kind did not exist. There are of course more mixed-race people around now, but back then I'd never even met a girl of "my kind."

School was generally a challenge for similar reasons. Despite all the efforts over the years, the U.S. has never gotten over its issues with race. Fortunately for me, I was an eclectic mix that allowed me to blend well with virtually any race bearing brown skin. In the schools I attended where the predominant minority was African-American, I would allow myself to be seen as black. Where there was a strong representation of both black and Latino, I'd allow any given individual's bias to stand. If someone assumed I was black, then to them I'd be black; if someone assumed I was Latino, to them I'd be Latino. As a kid you do what you feel you need to do to survive. I learned to be a chameleon, adapting to my surroundings, living within the eye of the beholder.

Some may find that to be less than honest, but I was a half-breed kid in a black and white world where those of us in the middle had little support. I made my way the best I could.

Growing up as mixed race was hard for all six of us. We never easily fit. But having a bunch of siblings who were just like me helped a lot. We loved each other, yes, but could we fight. That thirteen-year age difference from oldest to youngest meant there was always someone young enough to get on someone else's nerves. I remember any number of all-out knock-down-drag-outs we boys would have. Fists flying and lots of screaming. I'll never forget the fight I had with one brother that ended with me running away from him and him throwing a hammer that hit me in the back. Yet, as we fought and scrapped like normal (or not!) siblings, we knew we were unique in our world, and so to some extent we relied on one another. And the girls, my older sisters, were supportive even though they were off living their own adult lives.

We were always in some way the outsiders. Yet without fail, each time I came home in tears, either from the playground bullies or the girl who said her dad said I couldn't date her, Mom and Dad were there. And their words were always the same, filled with passion and unbending commitment: "You are ours. We chose you. We love you just as though we gave birth to you. You are our son. God made you incredibly special and we're so glad he gave you to us! And if those people don't like you, well, you don't need them. Go on, live your life and be the best you can be." The other language they would use, although not exactly curses, will not be repeated. Let's just say that you really don't want to cross my mother on this topic. It won't be pleasant. You see, I'm her special son and you are not.

My parents never left me wondering if they really loved me. They did, period. It was at their knee where I learned what it meant to be cared for by someone who wasn't your "family." As a matter of fact, I can honestly say that I can't remember a time when I wasn't aware of having been adopted. Nor can I recall a time when I ever felt my parents were anything less than my blood relations. Their honesty about my origins and their passionate love for me was always evident.

I did date throughout high school, but it was in Bible school where I met my partner and wife. We were seated alphabetically on the first day of class. She was an *F* and I was an *H*. (Thank god there were no *G*s!) So we met that day, and have now been married for over thirty-two years. Just in case you're curious: she is blonde and blue-eyed, can't spend too long in the sun, and is just my kind.

I've been taught a deep appreciation for the diversity in life. The fact that there are so many different skin tones in the world points to God's creativity and love of variety. I so completely believe that we are all made in God's image and that we each bear an indelible print of His likeness. Also, how truly boring the world would be if everyone looked just like me—it would be a fairly good-looking place, but you get my point.

I was forced early on to come to an understanding of the warped thinking some apply to life, to grow and mature in ways I otherwise might not have. And as in so many of life's difficulties, we have a choice in how we respond. I chose to see my self-worth through the eyes of my parents: that although my skin color may have been different from the majority of those around me, I remained a wholly loved and integral part of my family.

When you take a step back and view things with a wide-angle lens, the bigots quickly fade. What you see in the grand picture are two people who had so much love in their hearts that they took in six kids, made them their own, and gave them an honest shot at life. Daily they would remind those kids of the love they had for them and that they'd chosen them to be their children. So when you stop and consider this depth of love, does the hatred of others matter? It doesn't. It was these lessons learned early in life and the experience of consistent, dedicated, loving parents that I believe instilled in me the ability to persevere.

My entire life has been spent in church. I was there via the womb when my birth mom attended at the orphanage and then Sunday after Sunday on the "Let's Adopt a Baby" show. But it wasn't always a refuge. The first time I left a church was when the pastor visited my parents and told them that it really wasn't right that they had adopted a black baby. Mom and Dad took exception to his theology, and we moved on.

I've known from an early age that the world isn't always a caring and welcoming place, and that these frailties make their way into all spheres of human interaction—even the Church. Dad was a pastor for many years, and my parents' desire was that I, as the first-born son, would follow in his footsteps. (And I think it says something about my parents that they used that term to describe me.)

Let's just put it out there: I'd make a lousy pastor. If all a pastor had to do was speak on Sunday mornings, I'd probably make out pretty well. But that doesn't even scratch the surface. It's the board meetings, the people problems, and all the stuff that's all too often wrapped up in a glossy religious context that I have no patience for. The tendency for people to spiritualize the most trivial of concerns while ignoring vital issues drives me a little nuts. Then for me to be the leader who helps correct it all . . . Well, I simply haven't been called to, nor do I have the talents for, this work. When it comes to the Church, I've just about seen it all—the good and the bad. I'm the guy who could give you virtually every reason for not darkening the door of a religious institution. I have no desire to beat up on the Church, though, so I'll just say that it's made up of a bunch of imperfect people, like me, who can confuse faith.

However, I continue on in the faith of my parents despite the fact that the Church doesn't always get life right. In my experience, it took far too long to embrace race relations, and at times it still comes down on the wrong side of that issue. I'd have a tidy little nest egg tucked away if I had a dollar for every time I heard a preacher speak against mixed-race relationships. I carry on in my faith because its core story of adoption so resonates with my soul and its central figure exudes such unconditional love. My parents lived these attributes. They embodied what the faith was supposed to mean in a world that was cold, even hostile, to the plight of a half-breed baby boy born in the wrong place at the wrong time.

I learned from my parents that our role in life is to look after one another, whether that be emotionally, physically, or spiritually. They worked extremely hard to care for their nine children, and in turn to instill in us that ethic. We were taught that we were to earn our way in the world and not expect someone else to pave the path for us. It was our job to earn our keep and care for our wider community.

They taught us that our respect for humanity came from our God-given equality, for we were all loved equally. We were taught that skin color was a fact of life, not a basis for judging a person. It never made sense to me how people could dislike another based on the color of their skin.

As I grew up, I came to learn that skin color was just an easy target. It too easily allows us to differentiate ourselves, to create classifications. It becomes the hook we hang our fears on. Our fears in turn create an us-versus-them atmosphere in which we have someone to blame for our failures, someone to feel superior to, someone to take out our frustrations on. But it's all wrong. Anytime we allow our fears of "the other" to push us apart rather than being bold enough to come together, we fail each other. We fail ourselves. My parents proved six times over not only that we can come together but also that we can come together as family.

Looking back over the course of my life, I wonder if this is where the first seeds of my growth in perseverance were planted—in my birth mother's perseverance in seeing that I found a home and a shot at life, in my parents raising a brood of mixed-race kids. They persevered in the face of a sometimes unsupportive Church, in the face of an at times hostile larger community. In each case they took the long view and believed that their children could have, and deserved to have, a better life. And they never gave up on that reality.

This is the essence of perseverance that I want to explore together in this book. An almost indescribable belief that life can be better if only we stay in the race and persevere. A belief predicated on a life-altering thankfulness, a deep well of gratitude for my parents doing what no one else would. For being there when everyone else walked away. A gratitude I try to return by living to its absolute fullest the life that has been given to me.

An orphanage run by white people took in the half-breed baby boy of a white farm girl. A white man and woman made him their son and gave him a shot at life. With no assurance that he'd grow up to be a good kid or even love them in return, they took in someone no one else wanted. They ignored the conventional wisdom of the day and took what many considered to be a phenomenal risk. Who knew that that kid would have such an amazing life?

chapter 3

Winnipeg

I WAS EIGHTEEN WHEN WE MET in Bible school in Kansas. To this day I remember how I felt when I looked to my side at this gal from Canada sitting there in her purple glasses. There was a feeling of familiarity, a deep sense that I could be friends with this person. No, not romantic right at the start, but something special, certainly.

Sheryl and I became great friends; I resisted anything more. It wasn't until we stood together at the close of school and she told me she was leaving, going back to Canada, that the penny finally dropped: I'd been a fool. It was then and there, with my heart racing, mind swirling, and palms sweating, that I first realized I was in love. And I knew I didn't want her to leave, that I needed her to be in my life.

This was in December. I told her I wouldn't write often— I wrote daily. In February I made my first trek to this foreign land called Canada. I had no idea how, being so far apart, we could sustain any kind of relationship. During that first visit to the frozen north I discovered what real cold was like and that Sheryl hadn't lied about this "sport" called curling—it really did exist. It didn't take much time for us to begin the conversation about her moving back to Kansas City. Within the next year she did, and within another year we were married. I was twenty and she was twenty-two. We had no clue what we were doing, we were flat broke, and we were crazy in love.

Unlike many people, our first years together were incredible. Oh, we fought, and we had to learn how to fight well. By that I mean she came from a comparatively quiet family that took a reasoned approach to their fighting. I came from a group of yellers. In my family we would never walk away from a fight in order to cool down and be rational; we'd stand our ground and "talk" it out until there was resolution. Then we were friends again and would move on. So Sheryl and I did figure it out, and along the way learned this really cool concept of making up. It was almost worth picking a fight for!

In those early years we were rarely apart. We worked at the same job, and in fact we shared the same office. We were youth leaders with Kansas City Youth for Christ, a crazy fun job that kept us out all hours of the day and night. We could go days, literally, without ever being out of each other's company. I loved every second of it. During the school year we oversaw a number of youth groups in various schools. We would plan outings, lead Bible studies, go on trips, and mentor kids through their teenage years. On Saturday nights we'd help host a youth rally of a thousand-plus teenagers where we'd put on skits, show movies, and be entertained by the latest in the Christian music scene. It was a very cool job.

Of the many "jobs" we had while at Youth for Christ (YFC), one of my favorites was spending the summer at youth camp. It was a ridiculously fun way to earn a living: sitting by the pool, planning incredible adventures in the massive forested property, fishing and canoeing on a huge lake, all the while working with kids. It was a grand life.

During one of those summers we were presented with an out-of-the-blue dilemma. For a number of months a couple on staff had been fostering a baby girl named April, who happened to be African-American. One day they asked us whether we might consider adopting her. I was thunderstruck. First of all, I thought I was too much of a kid myself to consider having kids. Second, even though I was adopted, I'd never considered adopting a child myself. Growing up, I'd looked forward to one day getting married and having my own children, but with no particular reason in mind, never gave the question of adoption serious thought.

The story was that the state was having a difficult time finding a home for April, and so the good couple looking after her thought we might be interested and willing. Why they chose us has always been a bit of a mystery to me. I suppose in some ways it made sense, in that they knew us well and knew we wanted to have children one day. Perhaps I was also the only black person of their acquaintance, which is possible. But the thought terrified me. I didn't know if I was ready for kids. April was clearly going to have a much darker skin tone than mine, *and* she would have a white mommy. All I knew for sure was that she'd face every kind of discrimination that I had growing up. Could I subject her to that? And where were all the good Christian black families that should be stepping up to take her? I just didn't know if I could do it.

It wasn't as hard to convince Sheryl—she was ready to sign the papers practically on the spot. You may not be the praying sort or even believe in a higher power, but let me assure you that I spent a lot of time praying. The longer I prayed and the more Sheryl and I talked, the more I felt that it was the right thing to do. And the fact that this was all transpiring while we were alongside April's foster parents was amazing, since it meant we had the opportunity to see her pretty much every day. And the more I saw April, the more I knew that we needed to do for her what had been done for me: give her a chance at life. Sheryl and I had never discussed adoption, but we'd certainly discussed having children. And although we weren't planning to start a family at the time, we nonetheless felt that this was something we had to do.

So we said yes. Our hearts had wholly fallen in love with this little girl, and we would pursue the crazy idea of adopting her. Phone calls were made, expressions of joy were given, paperwork was begun and then signed. Everyone was thrilled that April would have a home.

Then it all fell apart. With no warning and with precious little explanation, she was simply taken from our lives. All we ever knew was that she'd been adopted.

April would be twenty-seven now. Our time together was brief and intense—so brief that it's not all that hard to push it from my mind. But when I do let memories of her float through my consciousness, the sadness, the disappointment, the anger can still flash hot. I understand more clearly now, but at the time it seemed like such a cruel joke that God had played on us. We had been taunted and left with broken hearts. With nothing so much as a simple explanation.

It took me a long time to understand what this moment in our lives was all about. The lesson did not come easily. I had stepped out, willing to do something that scared the daylights out of me in order to help this little girl, only to have it fall apart and see my wife left in tears.

During the adoption process, Sheryl and I had begun talking about the possible need for a bigger home. Our little two-bedroom, eight-hundred-square-foot starter house wasn't going to cut it. And now that the wall around the having-children conversation had been thoroughly breached, we began discussing the idea of having our own. With that question fully in play, we would indeed need to find a bigger house. So we set out on the hunt, and soon found the perfect one to make our home. It was so long ago that I don't remember much about it, except that it had a bay window facing east (I imagined watching the sunrise every morning over coffee) and that Sheryl loved it.

So we made an offer and put our first, modest little house on the market. The purchase of the new house depended on the sale of the old. And the old just would not sell. Once again we found ourselves in a situation where everything seemed so right, so perfect, and yet nothing would come together. It felt like an eternity as we anxiously waited for an offer that never came. Then someone else made an offer on the new house. We had something like seventy-two hours to produce the cash or lose the house we wanted so much. In a brief span of time I'd seen my young wife desperately disappointed twice. From then on, life in Kansas City was never quite right.

I'd been restless in my work before these events, even though there were many things about the job that I loved, including the many incredible people we worked with. Still, I had a sense that the time was coming to move on. I just had no idea what I would move on to. Aside from a bit of Bible school, I had no postsecondary education.

It was a difficult time for me, as I didn't want to go back to school. You will recall my lack of love for the education system. But the time came when I knew I needed to do something. Sheryl had an idea. Why don't we move to Canada for a while to be near her parents and family? In fact, there was a YFC office right there in Winnipeg that we might be able to transfer to. It had the smell of a good idea, but, twice burned by the prospect of a big change, I was wary.

We figured we'd push on a few doors and see what would happen. It began with me sitting down with my current employer and hashing out my concerns about my job. That did not go well, so we applied at the YFC in Winnipeg after all. The interview process was smooth, and my application was not only warmly received but also came with an offer of financial assistance to help us make the move.

After much deliberation and consultation with people who cared about us and whom we considered wise, we made the decision to go. There is no one to blame for what happened next. But you know the old adage, "Out of the frying pan and into the fire"? Yeah, our move was something like that. Nothing in my life had in any way prepared me for Winnipeg. In the four years we'd been married and the two years before that, I'd been in Canada ten or so times. I *felt* prepared. I'd seen the place and the people, experienced the cold, and I knew what I was getting in to. Only, I didn't. I had no idea that hell had frozen over.

I'd experienced minus-forty-degree weather, but I'd never lived in it. These Canadians who spoke the same language, lived in the same houses, wore the same clothes, and ate at the same McDonald's restaurants were not the same people as Americans. Possibly because I was so confident (naive?), the ensuing culture shock felt extreme. The work cultures of the two YFC offices couldn't possibly have been any more different from each other, too. I found myself out of my depth and feeling very alone.

It's probably a good time to note that Sheryl was now pregnant with Tim Jr.

And then the crème de la crème was the incessant imploring by friends and family in Kansas City to just admit our mistake and come back. But a minus-forty day in Winnipeg was a balmy tropical afternoon compared to the cold day it would have to be before I tucked tail and ran home in defeat. There was no chance of my giving up and going home.

When you line up the major life decisions we'd taken in a short period of time, it will come as no surprise that we began to struggle in our relationship. We had moved (changed countries!), were pregnant, had new jobs, and now had very few support systems. So after eleven months we decided to leave Winnipeg's YFC. It just wasn't working. In many ways we felt adrift.

Yet we had a firm conviction that we were on the path we were to walk. Even in our most difficult days we never really doubted the rightness of our decision to move. Now, that doesn't mean I liked it. As a matter of fact, at the time I hated Winnipeg and would have given anything to get out. But we became convinced that we were not to give up. That there was a reason for our being here. And every time someone suggested we admit defeat and move home, it solidified my resolve to do anything but that.

It was during this time that April and the second house started to make sense. We came to the conclusion that those difficult events were about trust. I appreciate that many don't see life through the same lens as we do, but we were convinced that God was taking us somewhere and that there were lessons to be learned. We came to see that these events were small, painful steps in a bigger lesson. I now believe that they entered my life as a way of preparing me to make the move to Canada. Being so young when I got married, I went from life at home with my mother to life at home with my wife—I was very content where I was. Both April and the house set me on a path of a certain discontent that allowed me the strength to move. Only in moving would I be challenged to grow, to mature, to become the person I needed to be. Only in moving would I ever encounter the reason for writing this book.

I hate discomfort. Yet all this discomfort has led me to a better place. I like to say that I was born in Texas, raised in Kansas, but grew up in Winnipeg. It's true. My character was challenged, my marriage was challenged, all that I thought I believed about faith and God was challenged. In short, it was by far the most difficult time in my life, rivaled only by being diagnosed with Parkinson's.

Yet I've learned that persevering pays off in spades. I look now at all I would have lost had I given up, and I shudder at the thought. We're often told that if something isn't making us happy, we should just drop it and move on. Trust me when I say that there were many days when I wasn't happy. Trust me when I say that I'm so very happy I didn't give up on any aspect of my life.

Sheryl and I now have a life that's filled with far more meaning. It is deeper, richer, has more color, and has been woven into a beautiful tapestry that we wouldn't have experienced had we simply pursued happiness. I think we've been sold a lie when we're told to pursue only those things that will make us happy. I can't express clearly enough how happy I am that I didn't give up on Sheryl, that she didn't give up on me, and that we didn't move home to Kansas—even though that may have been easier, and may have even made me happier, however briefly, at the time. I love Kansas but I needed Winnipeg. I needed to stay and grow through the pain into the person I had to become.

Sheryl and I doubled down on our life together. We accepted that life sometimes just sucks, but that we would see a better future. We didn't think of it in these terms at the time, but we did choose to do our best. We got up every day believing in each other, trusting in the decision we'd made. We would make a plan, alter it as needed, and keep putting one foot in front of the other. It took a long time and many hard days, but we can say that we built a beautiful life.

I've learned through firsthand experience, in hand-to-hand battle with life, that I can persevere and win. I've walked through life with an incredible partner who has my back, just as I have hers. I know what it feels like to force yourself to keep going even when you have no idea how you'll make it. And yet we made it.

And now there's Parkinson's. Really? There are days when I feel as though I can't do this. But then I'm reminded that we've already run this kind of race and won. We've been here before. Sure, the challenges aren't the same and this race will be longer, but I've tasted victory after a bitter trial and this will be no different.

I don't always feel it, I know I won't always hold my head up high in strength, and God knows there are days when I falter, but deep in the core of my soul there will forever live a little ember of hope and defiance that says to Parkinson's, "Bring it! I know this battle has already been won."

chapter 4

Uncovering History

WHEN DOES A CHILD REALIZE he's different from others? In my case, I always knew I was adopted. Still, I had no idea why my birth mother gave me up, why she was unable to care for me. As a kid you speculate all the time, of course. Yet in all our questioning—and I say "our" because these were family questions, not just my own—we never assigned blame. My parents were remarkably adept at helping us understand that since we didn't know the circumstances of our births, we were in no position to judge the decisions made on our behalf. Instead we chose to believe that the best decision possible had been made for us; we endeavored to leave the whys to God.

However, the not knowing leaves a gaping hole. Some deal with it better than others, and I've come to believe that there is little the adoptive parent can do to determine the child's response. As one of six, I've had the opportunity to view up close the range of emotional responses we've covered in our quest to understand ourselves more fully. Even though we were parented by the same people in the same house, we've all experienced this struggle differently. Some have grown up angry with what they have or haven't found, others are content with their discoveries, and still others have chosen to forgo altogether the search for knowledge about their births. The one constant has been our parents' love for us and our love for them.

Parents of adopted children have asked my advice on how to deal with telling their kids they were adopted. My reply has always been the same: be honest. As far as I'm concerned, it's hard enough knowing that you're adopted; I can't imagine what it would feel like to discover you've been lied to all your life. That may sound harsh, but no matter the good intentions, the child hasn't been told the truth. So my advice is to tell the truth and work out the details from there. If you're looking for an easier answer, I don't know one.

For adopted kids, my advice has been similar: be honest with yourself and your family. This isn't easy, and deserves attention. I always approached searching for my mother fairly realistically, I think. Early on I acknowledged that I might not like what I found if I went searching, that I wasn't guaranteed a happy ending. So if you don't like your current circumstances, please don't be so naive as to think that what you find will be any better. It may, in fact, be worse. Ask yourself some hard questions—like "How will I feel if what I find out is really bad, or makes me sad or angry?"—and then answer them honestly.

Me? I went looking. When my firstborn went cross-eyed at nine months of age, it lit a fire in me that I'd never experienced before. It was early in my nursing education, and I had to know why this was happening to my son. Medically speaking, I understood what Tim Jr. had, but I also knew that it was genetic. I simply had to find out where it came from. Although it was a fairly ordinary condition called "hyperopia," or farsightedness, his was severe enough that it caused his left eye to completely cross. It took little in terms of medical care to have it diagnosed and for baby Tim Jr. to be fitted with glasses before the age of one. He was a fabulous toddler with his new eyewear. With a funky little black strap attached to keep his glasses on, he never took them off before bedtime. I think his sight improved so dramatically that he actually enjoyed wearing them. And given how well it worked out, this new desire of mine bordered on irrational. I just knew I had to try to find my birth mother. For me the search had nothing to do with needing a mom— I had an incredible one already. I didn't need to somehow fill a void in my personal life; I was content with who I was and who I had become. I just wanted to understand my genetic history. Hardly heartwarming, I know.

So I set out on a quest that proved to be both short and sweet. Having only my birth certificate with my birth mother's name and a twenty-five-year-old address, I headed to the library in downtown Winnipeg. Once there, I accessed the white pages for her old home town via microfiche. (Yes, anyone under the age of thirty will need to Google that entire last sentence.) I found a number that appeared to hold promise. Now, I wasn't sure how someone on the other end of the phone would react to me calling out of the blue asking for the mother who gave me up as a baby, so I devised a plausible cover story. (I'm not comfortable with outright lying, but I think the circumstances justified some delicacy.) It wasn't exactly original—I claimed to be an old friend of my mother's from college, trying to reconnect. On calling the number listed, I reached a very pleasant woman who told me there was no one by that name in her clan (her word, not mine), but that I might try the clan over the way in the next town. Back to the microfiche to find any likely numbers. No one answered at the next one I tried. But the second number in the same town resulted in me speaking to my birth mother's brother, who bought my "old college friend" line and gave me her number. So, on the fourth dial of the telephone—four calls was all it took—I spoke to my mother who had given me up for adoption twenty-five years earlier.

I quickly but calmly explained who I was, the circumstances of my birth (as much as I knew about them), and my birthdate. Then I asked if this meant anything to her. Amid the tears there was a small "Yes." And thus I embarked on a new journey with a woman who would become a very dear, special friend and in many ways a second mom.

As to the genetic question, it turns out that my birth father had the same eye condition as Tim Jr., but in his case it had resulted in the permanent crossing of his right eye. With proper medical attention he could have had it corrected (as Tim Jr. did). But I suppose his economic or perhaps social circumstances had prevented him from having access to this intervention.

Some have asked if I've ever thought of looking up my birth father. Certainly I've thought about it. But he was a married man with children, so, no, I see no reason to rain down that kind of potential grief onto all our lives. I have a father, a dad, who has cared fabulously for me. I see very little upside in that kind of quest. Just imagine if I were a simple mistake, a one-off, where he never got involved and went on to live his life. What if his wife never knew, his kids never knew? Maybe he even has grandkids now, and suddenly I show up. To what end? What do I need so badly that could justify causing possible grief? Some might say that it's not fair, that he should own up, play his part, be held to account. I am fifty-two years old. I can promise you that life is never going to be fair. So I've chosen to forgo any potential upside. I've chosen to let it lie.

When I think about everything my birth mother went through, I can see that the seeds of perseverance were planted early in life. Being single, white, and pregnant by an older black man in 1964 was not an easy road to walk. Then, like many young women in her position, she was sent away in secret, alone, to have her illegitimate baby and then give it away. I think of the courage she must have had. I think about the fear that must have engulfed her life, the despair at finding herself alone in this situation, and I marvel at her strength of character. The strength that propelled her forward, that allowed her to persevere through this harsh time and give me life.

Knowing her as I do now, I can see how she made it. She's tough and caring, and that's all I really need to know. Of course she's told me about the events surrounding my birth. What I take away is a story of a young woman who knew the right thing to do for her baby and who was tough enough to see it through on her own. In the seemingly simple act of giving birth to me, she's taught me what it means to persevere.

The decision to pursue my birth mother and not my birth father has its own lessons in perseverance. We all love both our parents, but there's a special kind of need we have for our mothers. It's telling that when people first discover I'm adopted they'll ask if I've ever looked for my mother; generally, it's only later in the conversation that they'll ask whether I've looked for my father.

Yet in many ways it seems to be our paternal lineage that informs so much of how we see ourselves and that answers the question "Who am I?" Having little information about my father's family, I'm still left with a small question as to who I am. Yet my choice to leave this stone unturned has given me another opportunity to persevere in the decision I've made.

In part it comes down to that old adage about choosing your battles. How much of an upside do you anticipate, an upside for which you're willing to pay the price of a downside? For without a doubt, whichever direction you choose, there will be a price to be paid. So the question for me was, Which will have the lesser negative impact? I was motivated to seek out my mother by specific reasons, and was willing to accept whatever else that might bring into my life. I've chosen to forgo knowledge of my father with the assumption that this would be the less distressing choice for all concerned. Now I get to live with the decision.

My birth mom and I have now known each other for almost thirty years. Her name is Eleanor. Even though we live far apart, we have a wonderful relationship. We see each other once a year or so and speak often by phone. She has come to be an important part of my children's lives. We celebrate birthdays and holidays, much as we do with the other grandparents.

For many years my mother didn't know that I'd contacted Eleanor, for the simple reason that it would have upset her very much. I am her son—wholly—and there would be no sharing. But as we were living life, a funny thing happened along the way. Tim Jr. grew up and decided to get married. He knew and loved both his paternal grandmothers and wanted them both at his wedding. The day I had long dreaded was upon me: I was going to have to tell Mom about Eleanor.

It had to be okay though, right? I was a middle-aged man now, and my relationship with my mother hadn't changed over these many years—she'd always been my mom and always would be. She had to see that, right? Yeah, I was basically terrified of having this conversation.

I wasn't going to see Mom in person before the wedding, so our talk would have to happen over the phone. Besides, I felt safer that way. I told her the whole tale and she listened quietly, asking few questions until I was done. In the end there were really only two questions that mattered. The first was, Why had I waited so long to tell her? It took some discussion, but in the end we agreed that, earlier in life, she wouldn't have taken the news well. The second question was never asked, but it was answered nonetheless. Geneva is my mom—she always has been and she always will be. She took my startling news with all the grace, dignity, and understanding that I knew she possessed. She showed me again the quality of woman it takes to adopt and raise six biracial babies.

It was a terrific wedding. Mom and Eleanor got along fabulously, almost too well, if that's possible. I suddenly found them teaming up, jointly lecturing me (kindly), as mothers are wont to do. It was weird and wonderful all at the same time. And yeah, Tim Jr. and his bride, Kara, worked out nicely as well.

chapter 5

Early Onset

LIFE HAD SETTLED INTO A ROUTINE: raising Tim Jr., working, and going to school. Having left Winnipeg's YFC, and having decided that we wouldn't be moving back to Kansas City, I'd found myself in need of a career. Then, after stumbling through a few jobs, I came to the conclusion that, whether I liked it or not, I needed to get an education. Question was, What to do? I had a wife and a kid and needed a real future.

It took a fair bit of deliberation as to what direction to take. My natural inclination was to head toward a business degree, but job prospects seemed uncertain at best. At one point I was discussing my dilemma with my brother-in-law, and he asked if I'd ever considered nursing. Now, don't judge me, but I was a growing young man and in truth my first thought was, "No, that's a girl's job." At the same time, though, it intrigued me. Mom had always cared for elderly people in our home as a means of earning a living, and I'd always enjoyed that experience.

In the end, I decided I didn't care what some people might think: I would go join the women and become a nurse. My reasoning was practical. It was a two-year diploma program rather than a four-year degree. When you finished school you had a set job (some might even say a trade) to go into. Nurses, like other health professionals, were always in demand. It paid well, it had great benefits right out of school, and it was portable. Just in case the day ever came that I did want to return to the States, my job would have legs: it would travel.

I was one of the very few guys in my nursing class—at the time, men made up only about three percent of the nursing workforce in Manitoba. (So anyone judging my initial reaction, well . . .) Whatever the demographics, I've loved my nursing career; that decision proved to be one of the smartest ones I've ever made. It has provided me with a meaningful, stable, well-paying job. I've had the opportunity to be a bedside nurse (my favorite role), I've worked in an air ambulance, and I've managed a team in a hospital. It has been challenging and very rewarding. I can't imagine having made a better career choice.

By my second year of school I had my life planned out. After getting my diploma, I'd work and continue my education at the same time by taking an intensive care course. Once the ICU course was done I'd work for another year or two and *then* we'd go back to the States, where I would finish my nursing degree and likely pursue a master's. (I'd come a long way from kindergarten in my attitude toward education.) Meanwhile our second child, Jordana, came along. A blonde, brown-eyed, beautiful little girl. Life was looking really good.

Of course, life doesn't always go exactly as planned. I had trouble finding a nursing job right out of school, ending up working as a healthcare aide for a year and then as a nurse in home care for a year after that. Once I got back into the hospital, where I wanted to be, I took some time before applying for the ICU course. Then I discovered that I didn't enjoy ICU work. By this time Carter and Eleni, our twins, were born. I found myself with little time for more school and with no great desire to move back to Kansas. So we worked, raised our kids, and made a life. A good life.

Most Saturday mornings I get up and read the paper with a cup of coffee. It was while I was sitting in the kitchen, tucked away in our Starbucks-inspired reading nook, that a brand-new thought entered my mind. *My left big toe is twitching.*

Raising the paper just slightly, I looked down and sure enough my toe was twitching. All of its own accord, rhythmic and continuous. I could make it stop, but then it would just start up again. By now I'd been a nurse for eighteen years, and I knew that you don't wake up twitchy for no good reason. So I did what any nurse would do: a quick head-to-toe assessment. Perhaps it was psychological.

I'm not depressed or anxious, everything is good at work, the kids are okay, and all is well with my wife. Life is generally all right. There is really no psychological reason for me to be twitchy.

My thoughts carried me forward toward the conclusion that if this wasn't psychological then it must be physiological, and if it was physiological then it was likely neurological, and if that was the case then it was likely either multiple sclerosis or Parkinson's disease.

That was the first five minutes on my journey with this thing called Parkinson's.

July 2010 had marked our twenty-fifth wedding anniversary, and we had a three-week European holiday booked for October. I decided that the good-husband thing to do was to keep my mouth shut. Maybe I was wrong and the twitches would go away. I decided not to worry Sheryl with it. We would go on vacation and relax.

I've since learned that any kind of stress—good, bad, or indifferent—will make Parkinson's symptoms worse.

We had decided to do in our forties what should be done in one's twenties, which was to backpack across Europe. Our first hotel was booked in Madrid and our last hotel in Athens, with nothing in between. We were going to plan the trip on the fly. We each carried one backpack. With my inclination toward a five-star rather than a hostel experience and my preference for detailed plans, I was a bit stressed at the outset of our travels.

A word to the wise. Should you choose to take a similar trip, do not show up in Rome on a Saturday night without a hotel room booked. We made this mistake and found ourselves following a guy who knew a guy who had a great place available to stay for the night.

As we walked through Rome's dark alleys late in the evening, it occurred to me that if any of my kids did this and survived to return home, I would kill them. We had made a dumb decision. Fortunately for us, the little boutique hotel we were led to was lovely, though ridiculously expensive. However, it beat sleeping in the train terminal all night!

At some point during this little adventure the toe tremor turned into a foot tremor. That foot tremor then turned into a leg tremor. Finally, I broke down and told Sheryl about my concerns. It was clear that the symptoms were only getting worse. I was slowly getting worried that something might be seriously wrong with me.

Being the strong, confident woman that she is, Sheryl encouraged me to relax. Whatever was going on could be sorted out when we got home, and regardless, she was by my side and all would be well. With that, I settled down. We carried on having a fabulous time.

On our return home there had been no change in the tremor, so I went to see my family doctor. The two of us sat in his office for half an hour discussing the fact that I likely had what's known as young-onset Parkinson's. To do his due diligence, he would refer me to a neurologist for further examination. In February 2011 I was formally diagnosed with the disease.

I'd nursed many Parkinson's patients, so I had a clear understanding of what the diagnosis might hold for me. Plus, my father had died with this disease. Dad had been unwell for many years. He had his first heart attack at fifty-five, and things never really got better after that. He ultimately had three open heart surgeries, both carotids done, and innumerable angiograms. He eventually came down with diabetes and was later diagnosed with Parkinson's. Mom and Dad always held things close to the chest, and as a teen I wasn't as attuned to the subtle changes my dad was going through. But I vividly remember his frustration with the disease, his constant complaints that his insides were shaking. As the disease progressed he lost facial expression and his voice began to wane. Otherwise, honestly, Parkinson's never factored that highly in all the ailments Dad had. Only after I was diagnosed did I really begin to recall the now obvious Parkinson's symptoms he'd had. At the time, we as a family were far more concerned about his diabetes and cardiac problems. Now it all became relevant. I began to refresh myself on the technical aspects of the disease.

Parkinson's is a progressive neurodegenerative disease that results in the decreased production of dopamine in the substantia nigra portion of the brain. I love that sentence. It makes me sound smarter than I likely am. The straight-forward definition is that it's a disease that will get worse over time, guaranteed. Since there's no cure for it, my future health is reasonably well known and not altogether pretty.

Another way of defining it is that Parkinson's is a nerve disease of the brain. If you look right down through the center of the brain you'll find the thalamus, and right under that is the substantia nigra, whose job is to produce a chemical called dopamine. Parkinson's causes nerve damage in the substantia nigra, limiting its ability to produce dopamine. Dopamine is critical for the proper movement of our bodies.

Without dopamine our bodies present with a number of symptoms. The four classic ones are tremors (shakiness), rigidity (stiffness), loss of balance, and slowness. Less known are the nonmotor symptoms, such as anxiety, depression, and cognitive problems. Parkinson's is an insidious, evil sneak that slowly robs you of the ability to control your body.

When I received the formal diagnosis, I responded the way many do when they get bad news. I got depressed. I stopped running and riding my bike, and sat down on the couch. I stopped looking after myself.

Looking back over my journal now, I see that the cessation of physical activity on my part wasn't quite as abrupt as I remember it being. It was more of a slow decline. I'd been training for a sprint-distance triathlon, and continued that through the winter and early summer, when I ran the race. It was after the tri that I began to let my running and cycling wane. The tri had taken a lot out of me physically, and my "rest" period turned into an outright quit period.

My journal reveals a guy who just wanted to forget the whole diagnosis. I wanted to believe that it would somehow go away, that the doctors would be proven wrong, or that I could set it on a shelf and ignore it. I think in many ways the family's response followed mine. We discussed it, but we made every effort to go on with life as though it didn't exist. This may be healthy in some ways, but in other ways it's not.

I found that Parkinson's could not be ignored. At one point in my journal I wrote, "I'm either constantly shaking or if I'm not I'm thinking about when the shaking will come back." It is unrelenting, rarely completely out of mind, and impossible to ignore. Thus, in some ways, I simply shut down. I had this bizarre sense that if I just sat still, held myself still, somehow the shaking would stop altogether. Of course, it did not. It never will.

After a year of this I finally shook my head and decided it wasn't the way I wanted to live. Nor was it the way I wanted to respond to this disease. In time, I returned to running and cycling and began to look after myself again. I got up, got going. I set some new goals, which included aiming for an Olympic-distance triathlon. That turned out to be a little too ambitious, but I did continue to run and cycle. I'd always enjoyed my ride to work: I had to go to work anyway, so why not bike? It was satisfying in a number of ways. It gave me a specific destination and allowed me to challenge my time every day. I even enjoyed riding throughout the Winnipeg winter—as crazy as that sounds. The exercise was phenomenal, and I'd never been in better shape physically.

This time was incredibly challenging because I was still early in the disease and far more was changing in my body than I was aware of or willing to acknowledge. My stamina was waning; even though I was determined to not let Parkinson's take any part of my life, I could sense it eating away at the edges. My emotional health was just starting to be affected, too, but there was no way under heaven I was going to admit that something like that could be going on.

I chose to embrace Parkinson's. I was determined to set my own rules and beat this thing. I was not, however, completely honest with myself about my circumstances. I continued to try to believe that I could ignore it and just go on. To my credit, I did for a fair while. I hunkered down, kept running, pushed my biking, and did my level best to embrace the moment.

From time to time I've been asked what Parkinson's feels like. Imagine that a small handle has been attached to your breastbone. Now imagine someone grabbing that handle and shaking it fast and steady, so fast that it's almost a vibration. It's not so hard that it shakes your whole body, but just hard enough that your skeleton shakes inside your skin. Eventually it progresses to shaking your body visibly.

To date, my Parkinson's has progressed to involve all of my left side, from my big toe up to my shoulder and occasionally the left side of my face. The tremor, and even the bit of rigidity that has set in, are generally manageable. I continue to walk rather than run, I bike some, and I do yoga, which are all incredibly helpful in managing my symptoms. I also attend Rock Steady Boxing classes—a noncontact, boxing-inspired exercise program for people with Parkinson's that has been great for me both physically and mentally. The camaraderie of fellow fighters beating the crap out of a heavy bag is fantastic. I remain hopeful that one day I'll be able to return to running. However, Parkinson's affects more than just the body. It's the anxiety and depression that I find most challenging to deal with. And these nonmotor symptoms are what ultimately led to my departure from my day job.

I often like to joke that the reason for leaving work was my patients' discomfort when I'd approach them with a needle while shaking. In truth, I was in management and doing very little direct patient care when the time came to retire. The fact was that life had been slowly stacking up on me; I was losing the ability to keep all the balls in the air. I'd been a nurse for over twenty years, and for the last number of these I'd worked in a high-stress position referred to as "bed utilization." Hoping to relieve some of my Parkinson's symptoms, namely anxiety, I thought I would change roles within the hospital, and so I applied for and received a position as a unit manager on a surgical ward. I was enjoying this new role, but then it became necessary to take on the management responsibilities of our operating room as well. The change can be described in six letters: stress. It didn't take long for me to begin to regret having made the change. No one can be blamed for these circumstances. At times life just deals you a complex hand, and this one ultimately proved too much for me.

Not that I didn't have great help. If not for the phenomenal group of people who surrounded me during this time,
I wouldn't have lasted as long as I did. The encouragement I
received came from the highest levels of the hospital right
down to those I worked side by side with every day. Most
weren't aware of the struggle I was having. I'd shared my
circumstances with my boss, but even then not fully. Looking
back, in some cases I wish I'd been more forthright and open
about what I was going through. Part of the reality, though,
was that I really didn't fully understand what I was experiencing or how to articulate it. I owe a debt of gratitude to my
colleagues at the St. Boniface General Hospital in Winnipeg.

In the midst of all this, I also had a family to care for. The
many and ongoing responsibilities of being a father, grand-
father, and husband. Yes, a grandpa! Tim Jr. and Kara blessed
us with our first grandchild four months before I left work.
Now, there's really no stress in this (how could there be?). But
I did want to be a good grandpa; I wanted to be around for
the long haul for this little one. And, of course, there was
always my new friend Parkinson's. People would often ask
me how I could do it, but the fact was that I just felt I could.
The work, the family, the intense exercise—for the most part,
it was all lots of fun. I like being busy; I enjoy the rush, the
chase, the thrill when it all goes well and you know you've
accomplished something special.

First there was that day when I realized that my left big
toe was twitching and how this was not a good thing. Then
came a similar day when I was sitting in my office at work and
had a new realization. The thought crept into my mind just
as abruptly: "I don't think I can do this anymore. I don't think

I want to do this anymore." It scared me because I'd never had a thought like it. I've always felt that I can do anything *and* take on whatever else that comes. I knew something was changing, but I charged ahead nonetheless.

That is, until I found myself sitting on a psychiatrist's couch, crying, trying to explain to him that I didn't know what was wrong and couldn't figure out why I couldn't keep up. He began to explain in more clinical terms what I'd already heard on many occasions. Maybe that's what the nurse in me needed to hear.

For me, the issue was anxiety and depression. I just couldn't handle my job anymore. Between the surgical floor I managed and the operating rooms I was covering during their manager's absence, I had more than two hundred employees under my care. This in a busy tertiary-care center of four hundred and fifty beds. It was my first such role, and it was challenging. But with Parkinson's, I found that the sheer volume of information needing to be handled was overwhelming.

It's an odd and scary aspect of Parkinson's. You can laugh and talk, walk, and function as though everything is normal, but all the while your mind is overwhelmed to the point of breaking. For a long time I had no idea how to think about what I was experiencing. In nursing school I hadn't enjoyed my psych rotation; I just trudged through it. Now I was terrified at the prospect of needing that knowledge.

I spoke to precious few about what was going on and just tried to cope. In time I simply couldn't. There were times when I'd be so overwhelmed with the volume of work facing me that I'd get completely lost. I'd call Sheryl in tears, asking her what work she thought I should do first. It was all unraveling.

Eventually, over the course of many months, I accepted the counsel of my neurologist and began seeing a psychiatrist. It's one of the best decisions I've ever made. At first I couldn't believe I was in this place emotionally and refused to accept it, let alone go to a shrink. It made no sense to me. I had always been strong. I could stand and give a speech, verbatim, from memory and know exactly where I was and where I was going at any point in the text. Now I was having days when I could barely string two sentences together.

And then there were those dark days when I could barely (and some days didn't) get out of bed: I'd feel convinced that all was lost, that the world was a dark and lonely place, that Sheryl would leave me and I'd die a lonely, broken man. It was at the end of one of these periods when the nurse's voice inside me made its way through all the chaos and implored me to get help. I remember that voice saying that if this were a heart attack I wouldn't waste a moment in seeking out a cardiologist, if this were a stroke I'd seek out a neurologist. If I wasn't quite broken emotionally, I was certainly in the process. So why would I not seek help in this matter?

Eventually, my doc came around to saying what my other doctors had been suggesting for some time: that I was doing too much, and needed to decide what was most important in life and pursue those things. There was a day not too long before when everything I had on my plate wouldn't have been too much. But Parkinson's was changing my life, and I was slowly coming to accept what was obvious to others.

I had to take stock and make some hard decisions. It was a bitter time. Yet, since I was mostly very tired, in a small corner of my being there rose a little cheer. After a difficult period of consultation with my healthcare providers and much dialogue at home, I chose to take a medical leave from work, which was the first step in pursuing long-term disability. This remains the most difficult decision I've ever made. The stress, anxiety, and feelings of guilt that accompanied it were at times all but unbearable. I would never have imagined myself being in this kind of awful position.

After several months of counseling, coming to terms with my disease state, and gaining a clearer understanding of what Parkinson's was doing to me, Sheryl and I made the decision that I'd retire from nursing. I knew it would make little sense to my colleagues; I'd been adept at keeping my struggles from them. Of course, there are all the other stereotypes we feel we'll be tagged with in dealing with mental illness. But I made the call and stepped out into the next chapter. It had been four years and ten months from the time of my diagnosis, and it was the right thing to do.

For me, counseling was one of the most difficult forms of help—not in itself, but in the guilt and pride I had to overcome in seeking it out. In my mind's eye I wasn't and never would be an emotional weakling. Men in my world did their jobs; they did not give up; and they certainly did not succumb to mental weakness. You pulled yourself together, got your head straight, and did what was needed. Until I just couldn't anymore.

I needed to attend sessions over only a few months, but it was some of the most helpful work I've ever done. I'm not sure I can be as articulate about this phase of my journey as I might like, but I suddenly found a freedom to explore issues that I'd never before discussed, out loud at least. I was free to be emotional. I was free to be weak and vulnerable and to investigate how all these feelings played into how I view myself and the roles I hold in life. Now, this is not to say that I have no other spaces to be vulnerable, but rather that this was a unique space for me: a freedom, guided by a caring professional, that gave me license to make discoveries about myself that I don't think I would have made otherwise. Just as a cardiologist helps our hearts heal, my psychiatrist helped my mind heal.

There were other things that helped me through this process as well. One was my dad. Although he passed away some seventeen years ago, I still take a lesson from his life. Having suffered from chronic cardiac disease, diabetes, and Parkinson's, he was never able to care for himself to a degree that may have extended his years beyond the seventy-two he lived. The last fifteen years of his life were very difficult for both him and our family. To the best of my ability I will choose to take care of myself with the hope of extending both the quality and quantity of my life for those who love me. I don't blame my dad for his difficult health; he was a product of his day. Getting a kid off the farm to change his eating habits proved extraordinarily difficult. However, I learn from his trials.

Another thing that helped me greatly is that I'm a nurse and I know better. I know that we as humans have a finite number of resources at our physical disposal. No matter how much I don't like it, Parkinson's eats into those resources and depletes them much faster than in an individual without the disease. It just won't allow me to do all that I'd want. I have to prioritize and organize my life, much as I did when caring for a complement of five or six patients.

When I worked on a busy medical or surgical floor, one of the most important aspects of good care was the ability to think critically and make good assessments. I could race around, chasing all the myriad tasks I had to do on a given day, or I could critically assess what was most important and do those things first. I finally figured out that I needed to apply that same thinking to my life. And when I did, it didn't make life easier, but it did make it better. I now knew what was most important to me and my family. I could set aside until later what was less important, and some things simply had to go.

I've learned to maximize the use of my personal resources, which has resulted in a greater return on investment, if you will. My shareholders (family) are happier, and in general I'm much more at peace. I have simplified and focused my life. By doing so I'm more engaged in the activities I choose to take on, and therefore see better results. It's been some time now since I've experienced one of those despairing days when I was curled up in my darkened room, unable to get out of bed.

I've also come to accept the reality that I'll likely never run another marathon (or half marathon for that matter). I'm okay with that now, mostly. I'll run what I can while appreciating the fact that I can run at all. I'll hold on to the memories of when I could finish a half under two hours, and as I remember, I'll smile. Those were the good old days—but they're not as good as the ones still to come. I'm learning to let go of the regret about what I can't do and hold on to the hope of what can still be done.

I'm learning to give myself permission to be this new me. Some days I have lots of energy and feel almost "normal." Those days are few. Therefore, most days I set a few specific goals, and when they're achieved, I accept that my workday is over. It's not easy—there are many things in life I'd still like to accomplish—but, in an ironic twist, the more I let go the more I seem to get done. And as I give myself permission to do less, it seems that what does get done is of a much better quality. I actually tend to finish things more quickly because I'm not distracted by all the other items I've deliberately set aside. As life has continued to roll forward, I've been amazed by what this practice of simplicity has produced and the good that has come from it.

I've never liked the idea of multitasking; it didn't make sense to me. I could work quickly and move seamlessly from one task to another, but I could never do two tasks at once. Parkinson's has driven home this reality. Some days I have a tough time concentrating on a single task, let alone the added physical struggle that results from my tremor. So I'm learning in a new way what it means to think about one thing at a time and do only that thing. It's a principle that I'm applying at home, in my work, in my writing, and in my interactions with others.

It turns out that this practice has the same positive results in my private world as it did in my nursing career. I'm more focused and less frantic; I experience less anxiety, and feel that I'm being more productive. From time to time the patients I looked after would thank me for my care and composure. Let's call that customer satisfaction. Now I'm finding that same customer satisfaction at home. I'm able to be a better father, husband, and friend. The people I care about have a better version of me around when I practice this type of simplicity.

Dopamine is often referred to as our "happy" drug. It's what produces that runner's high and what helps boost our moods in general. I am now in increasingly short supply of that drug. Parkinson's looks different on everyone, and this particular aspect seems to affect me perhaps more than some others. I hate it, but I'm coming to terms with it. I guess you could say I'm persevering with this aspect of the disease. I've embraced it, learning to understand it and thereby fight back against it.

Simplifying life reduces the stress and the anxiety, which in turn seems to reduce the depression. It would seem to follow that if you reduce these stressors you'd then reduce the demands made on your body for dopamine. Now, I have no objective data for this point, but as a nurse, I'd take an educated guess that I'm moving in the right direction here.

Although there is currently no cure for Parkinson's, there are some medications and surgical interventions that help moderate or reduce its symptoms. The gold-standard treatment is the use of a pill that goes by various names: the most common form is Sinemet, but I use Levocarb. This small yellow pill's goal is to replace some of the lost dopamine—a difficult task given that the brain has been built with a strong wall around it (the blood–brain barrier) for protection. Our brains are very sensitive and don't tolerate change well.

Around the globe, some of the brightest minds are looking for ways to improve the day-to-day lives of people living with Parkinson's. Researchers are putting in tireless efforts toward finding a cure. I cheer on the work of these individuals and hope that breakthroughs will be made in my lifetime. Meanwhile, whenever that cure or new treatment comes, I'm making sure that I'll be the healthiest person in line for it.

chapter 6

They'll Love Your Parkinson's

OF ALL THE THINGS that Parkinson's brought into my life, there's one that I'm so very grateful for: the disease got me on the very first season of *The Amazing Race Canada*. They say we should always look for a silver lining. Well, this was one massive bit of silver.

For the uninitiated, *The Amazing Race Canada* is essentially a traveling scavenger hunt. The teams (nine in our season) race across the country looking for a variety of clues and performing various tasks. We got to travel from coast to coast to coast, even to the shores of Hudson Bay in the north.

In the American version of the show, and in subsequent seasons of the Canadian version, the race takes place all over the world. But in season one we had the incredible opportunity to stay within Canada and explore parts of this great country I'd never seen before. I'd never even traveled east of Toronto, but during the show we visited all three territories and seven of the ten provinces.

The rules were simple. At the beginning of each leg of the race we were provided with a clue as to where we were to go. Each team was then responsible for getting themselves to that destination. Along the route there were a number of tasks to be performed, sometimes by one member of the team and sometimes both. It required ingenuity, smarts, and the occasional dose of good luck.

The teams were made up of individuals who had a prior relationship: father and son, best friends, spouses, and so on. At the end of each day the last team to arrive at the final destination would be eliminated from the race and sent home. That is, unless that day was a non-elimination round. On those days the last team to arrive would be spared, but would have an extra task to perform the following day—and that extra task all but ensured their elimination.

I like to say that I got on the race because of my Parkinson's and that we survived the race in spite of it. To my mind, Parkinson's and the race will be forever intertwined. The race, for me, is a story of embarrassment, loss, and redemption. Of Parkinson's and perseverance. And how I got to be a part of it all is thanks to one special person.

Blonde hair, soft blue eyes, a trim build. Quiet in all respects, at least in comparison to me. I've often described Sheryl as being "low maintenance." I'm hoping, as I write this, that she sees that as a good thing. To meet her you might not imagine how deeply her passions run, but therein lies a still, vast river. She is passionate about her children and about her faith, and believes that life should be lived through experiences rather than things. I suppose this is what drew her to watching *The Amazing Race* in the first place. She loves to travel. If I buy her expensive jewelry, I'll be in trouble. But if I book a week-end away somewhere exotic . . . well, different story.

She always said, "If the race comes to Canada, we're going to apply." Sheryl has watched every leg of every episode produced in North America. She's an avid fan, passionate, addicted.

The whole thing had come about by random chance or divine intervention. Her sister introduced us to an international student, Rafa, who was looking for a place to stay in Winnipeg while attending school. Tim Jr. had just moved out, leaving us an extra room. Sheryl approached me with the idea of having a complete stranger of a man come live in my house and eat my food. He was far from home, Mexico, and we could be of help to him. I said no. I still had two daughters living at home and didn't care to have some guy roaming around the house with them. Besides, I like my space, and that now-empty room meant I could finally have the office I'd been hoping for.

He moved in a few weeks later. Did I mention Sheryl's passion? Soon after moving in, Rafa introduced her to this reality travel show that had people racing all over the world competing for half a million dollars in cash and prizes. Sheryl fell in love with the show's destinations and the competition it involved. She was hooked, and soon introduced the show to me. I am so thankful for that passion.

In time, this American-based race did come to Canada and, true to her word, Sheryl was determined to apply. Being the skeptical yet dutiful husband that I am, I rolled my eyes and said, "Yes, dear." She dove into researching what it would take to enter and soon came back with the sad news that we couldn't: the race, she explained, would require us to be away for an extended period with little to no contact back home. Our oldest daughter was off traveling alone around Southeast Asia, but our twins were almost fifteen, and no one in their right mind leaves their fifteen-year-old twins at home alone for any length of time.

"Okay, dear," I dutifully replied. I didn't know anyone who'd ever made it onto a television show and didn't anticipate that I would, either. Who wins that kind of lottery anyway?

Sheryl took my eye roll in stride, but started a fight anyway. There was another way to go. Tim Jr. and I could apply.

I didn't see why, of the two of us, it should be me to apply with him. My argument was that since this was her dream, she should be the one to pursue it. Her argument was much more detailed.

She put forward that the race loves family teams. I pointed out that that would work for either of us. She countered that they'd love the fact that we're both named Tim, that we look so similar, that we'd both look great on camera (see what she did there?), and that they would love my Parkinson's.

That last point stopped me cold. In fact, it made me slightly angry. This piece of the conversation kept coming up over the next number of days as we discussed the idea of applying for the race. I was put off by the thought yet couldn't quite identify why. Was it that Parkinson's was altogether a bad thing, and so how could anything good come out of it? The idea that Parkinson's could be the catalyst for such a good thing left me feeling slightly used somehow. I suppose there was also a part of me that never wanted to be grateful in any way for having been given this disease. Even if it got me on the show, how could I be?

Sheryl pointed out that the race often involved individuals with particular challenges, such as having overcome cancer and the like. Since she'd seen every show, she knew they'd never had someone with Parkinson's and was convinced that it would catch their attention.

The argument carried on over the course of a number of weeks and would always come back to Sheryl's pointed assurance that they'd love my Parkinson's. I was continually frustrated by this. Was I a monkey in a zoo to be put on display? Was I to be ogled like the bearded lady of circuses gone by? I certainly had no desire to be pitied or humiliated.

The more we discussed it, the more absurd I felt the conversation really was. Yet this wasn't a passing fancy of Sheryl's, nor had she come up with the idea out of the blue. She had literally talked about it for years, and genuinely wanted us to apply. So I began to think about it all more rationally. What if we applied and didn't get on the show? That wouldn't be so bad. What if we did get on? Sure, it would be incredibly fun. Of course we'd love to have the money and the prizes if we won. Yeah, it would be really cool to be on TV. And, maybe . . . maybe it could be a positive somehow for Parkinson's.

But while I was pondering all this, I was missing something important. Sheryl was and is passionate about this race. It was her idea and her dream to run it. She'd seen the bigger picture, she understood something about the race that I never did, and she got the fact that Tim Jr. and I might have a real chance of getting an interview. She wouldn't apply herself, she said, because I would have a better shot. There are few people I know who would let go of their dreams to let someone else run with them. In the end, though, she remained a critical and very real part of the team. Her wisdom would make all the difference.

With the decision made, we set about making our audition video. (What? You thought the argument would continue, that I had some hope of winning it? Besides, she'd made some good points.)

The rules called for the submission of a three-minute video explaining why we thought we should be in the race. In short, two brown men in toques, scarves, and boxer shorts in the snow worked for us. It was Tim Jr.'s idea to lead in with a chilly yet eye-grabbing intro and then simply tell our story about Parkinson's. So we stripped down to our boxers, donned the aforementioned winter attire, and proceeded to make our video. Rafa was our cameraman; he shot our story with a Sony Handycam. Over the course of a bright, sunny Winnipeg morning, in about minus-fifteen-degree-Celsius weather, we shot two or three takes telling the producers of *The Amazing Race Canada* why we thought we deserved to be on the race.

The making of the video turned into a family affair, with everyone having an opinion on the script. The girls helped with hair (even though we were wearing toques). Decisions had to be made as to which toque and scarf each of us would wear, which mitts we'd put on, whether our boxers should match. Then came the arguments over whether we needed additional takes. It seemed it was never going to be good enough to satisfy everyone. Finally, I called the project done: no more. Besides, in my heart I knew that, even though we were having a great time, it was really just an exercise in futility. Rafa led the effort in editing, and once done, we shipped it off and I forgot about it. I had absolutely no expectation that we'd ever hear back. It was a fun day and the thought of being on the show was exciting, but no, it wasn't going to happen.

Sheryl and I have been married a long time, and I've come to appreciate that she often has a clearer take on things than I do. Still, I was taken aback when she said one day, "I guarantee you that you guys will get an interview." I still can't believe she called this. Not to mention that, like most husbands, I'm rankled when she's so right and I've gotten it so wrong.

I'll never forget that day the phone rang. It was the race, informing me that our video had been selected for consideration. I was sitting at my desk at work, and it took some time for me to collect my thoughts. The most improbable of phone calls had just happened. A team was going to be in Winnipeg, and we had a date and a time for an interview. I called Sheryl and Tim Jr. to tell them the news. I don't recall her ever saying the words, but we both knew she'd told me this would happen. That proved to be the first of many speechless moments for me along the course of the race, and anyone who knows me will tell you it's awfully hard to leave me speechless.

Ten thousand teams from all across Canada applied to be on season one of the race. And remember: I'd been truly opposed to having Rafa live with us, and I genuinely did not want to apply for the race without Sheryl because it was her baby. When you consider these barriers alone, it's amazing we ever saw the start line. And I got into the race, I won this lottery, because of Parkinson's. It takes a bit of effort to get your head around that.

Then consider that, of the roughly one hundred thousand people in Canada living with Parkinson's, only about ten percent are diagnosed before the age of fifty. A ten percent shot at anything is a pretty slim shot. If the doctor told you that you had a ten percent chance of dying during surgery and a hundred percent chance without it, you'd opt for the surgery. Conversely, if you bought a ticket for a fifty-million-dollar lottery that had a ten percent chance of payout, you'd be unlikely to sell the house and prepare to move to the Caribbean.

Yet in the course of two and a half years I won two lotteries that no betting man would have taken the odds on. Would I make it onto a travel-based reality show? No. Would I be diagnosed with a chronic, progressive disease in my forties? No. There was no reason in the world to think either of these things would happen, yet they did. And, of course, the one wouldn't have happened without the other. It's highly unlikely that I'd ever have made it on the show if I hadn't had Parkinson's.

I've always tried to live well, to look after myself and my family. I've always been physically active and, I believe, a hard worker. It seems that this has paid off for me when it comes to Parkinson's. When I was diagnosed, one of the first things my neurologist said was, "You're in as good a position as you could hope for with this disease because of the exercise you've done all your life." Ironically, I'd always told my friends that I was a runner because I was running from cardiac disease. Life is preparing us for the journey we will walk if only we pay attention.

I've heard "knowledge" defined as a collection of information and "wisdom" as the ability to accurately use it. Sheryl is the type of person who retains infinite amounts of knowledge in what she refers to as the "acres of space" in her head. She's also infinitely wise, and before the start of the race she shared with me a bit of that wisdom. Without it, we would likely have lost the whole thing at the end.

chapter 7

Don't Embarrass Us!

WHEN I WOKE UP ONE MORNING in downtown Toronto's Fairmont Royal York hotel, I knew I was living the dream because there was no way I could have afforded this hotel on my salary as a nurse. The bathroom was the size of my living room, personal house shoes and massive bathrobes were laid out, and given the thread count of the sheets, they hadn't been purchased at the local Walmart. The in-room dining menu revealed that I'd need a month's worth of lunch money just for breakfast. It was a shame I couldn't share this with my wife, but then again, it had been her idea in the first place.

It was remarkable how fast time had flown since the moment I received that phone call from the producers. We were first contacted in February and now, at the beginning of May, we were about to begin shooting. During those short few months we'd binge-watched almost every previous season of the show. We took notes along the way, we strategized, we dreamed of glory. But the most important piece of information we gleaned came from Sheryl's constant imploring that we pay attention as the race progressed.

On this first morning of our adventure, I awoke to the voices of our almost-fifteen-year-old twins ringing in my ears. "Dad, whatever else you do on this trip, please Don't Embarrass Us!" There's nothing like a set of twins to dim the experience of a luxury hotel. My mind came crashing back to reality. No longer was I lost in the dream where I have infinite wealth, where this was just another day on one of my many global jaunts overseeing my vast empire, where I was about to jet off to my next board meeting. No, with the help of my youngest, I was reminded that I'm a nurse by day and a father of four who's more often than not scraping by to make ends meet.

But really, I'm not complaining. Having raised four of my own, I'm fully aware that it's a responsibility of children the world over to hold their parents' egos in check. And, of course, it was only natural that my waking thoughts turn first to my children's mental well-being. Far be it from me to embarrass them on national television on purpose. The truth is, I didn't want to embarrass myself, full stop.

Even putting aside the twins' "encouragement," we had an inauspicious start. Before the race even began I made my first mistake and inflicted no small amount of self-imposed stress. During our very limited free time, Tim Jr. and I had decided to go for a short swim. For some reason I kept my waterproof watch on, which is something I never do. It leaked. And since Tim Jr. hadn't brought a watch, we had no timepiece. This was critical. Teams were responsible for getting themselves up in the morning and being where they needed to be on time; otherwise, they'd be left behind. We had to find an alarm clock to have with us on the race.

So to all the armchair quarterbacks out there who've sat at home wondering why the racers just can't seem to get their acts together, this is one small example. I was consumed with figuring out how to get an alarm clock. You see, we had no money, and even if we did, we couldn't go shopping (all part of the mystery of the show). We weren't able to wander about, so what to do about a watch?

Being the relatively unsophisticated guy that I am, I'd never stayed in a hotel like the Royal York. It turns out that if you just ask, they'll accommodate virtually any need you have.

If you've seen the Disney version of *Beauty and the Beast*, you may recall the character of Cogsworth the clock. We had in our room a nice little battery-operated alarm clock that was reminiscent of Cogsworth. So it dawned on me to make what I considered to be a ridiculous request of our housekeeper: Could we have the clock? "Sure," he said. I was shocked that our problem could be solved so easily. Then I panicked. What if the show's production people spot the clock and think we've stolen it? Well, I decided to follow Mom's advice and tell the truth. I pulled a member of the staff (whom we referred to as "bearded Mike") into the room and explained the situation. All was deemed acceptable, and the Tims (as we were known) had an alarm clock: Cogsworth II. Let the games begin.

Shortly before the start of the race we were introduced to our fellow competitors. There was Ears, as we referred to Brett and his wife, Holly, who together came to be known as the Doctors. There was BodyBreak of ParticipACTION fame, Joanne McLeod and Hal Johnson; the Girls, Celina and

Vanessa, a set of young, attractive sisters; the Hippies (who hated the nickname), a dating couple from B.C.; the Twins, another set of sisters who are identical twins and to this day I can't tell apart; the Cowboys, two gay friends from Alberta; and Brawn 1, or Dave and Jet; and Brawn 2, Jody and Cory. Jody was a sniper in the Canadian Armed Forces who'd lost both his legs from the knees down while serving in Afghanistan.

From Toronto we headed to Niagara Falls, which turned out to be the starting point of the race. Our first task was to find a butterfly conservatory and locate our next clue. Having found the butterflies, we took our clue and headed off. Sounds like a solid start; however, although we were the first to arrive, we were the last to get our clue. We'd made a wrong turn once there and allowed all the other teams to get into the conservatory before us. So when we did arrive, only one lonely clue remained; all the rest had been taken. Even worse, it turned out that the last clue had a partner, and that we should have taken both: one clue for each team member, just as we'd been instructed. First day, first task, first mistake.

From Niagara we made our way via Air Canada to beautiful Kelowna, British Columbia. Since I'm not a big fan of water, Tim Jr. took on the first substantial task of the race by gearing up to go deep-sea diving in Okanagan Lake in search of the mysterious Loch Ness–type monster called Ogopogo. Donning a metal helmet and scuba gear, Tim Jr. dove in. Once he'd found Ogopogo and our clue, we were on our way.

From Okanagan Lake we headed for the hills and to a train bridge overlooking a spectacularly beautiful ravine. It was here that I gave the cameras the first great opportunity to truly embarrass me. On arrival, Tim Jr. and I jumped out of our truck and raced toward a van that was to take us to our next location. As we approached, another team jumped into the van and it sped away. I could only assume that we'd been deliberately left behind, and so, in my frustration, I took off my backpack and threw it at the retreating vehicle. As it turned out, the van could carry only two teams at a time. There were two teams in the van. Not one of my finest moments. Tim Jr. succinctly pointed this out with a "That's mature, Dad." Fortunately for us, that scene was left on the cutting-room floor.

In time, the van returned and took us where we needed to go. Since I was up for the next challenge, I strapped on a harness and prepared to walk a twelve-inch-wide plank suspended far above the ground. My first thought was, "This does not look safe!" The spectacular location was lost on me as I peered over the protective rail. In what seemed to be hundreds of feet below lay a beautiful ravine covered in evergreens. The sounds of a distant stream made their way up the sides of the bridge on this lovely sunny day in British Columbia. What held my attention, though, was an extension ladder lashed to a rough-hewn pole in the bridge's support structure. Correction, make that two ladders strapped to the bridge, one slightly overlapping the other where they came together top to bottom. My instruction was to climb over the protective railing of the bridge, mount the ladder, and make my way—a very long way—down to a small platform. Once again, was this *safe*?

I had a tight-fitting helmet, a harness, and a secure line attaching me to the bridge. Still, this was not a comfortable position. I was worried about shaking and falling off. I'm not afraid of heights, but this was a little ridiculous. At the bottom of the ladders a plank was suspended out into space by a few cables. I could see it swaying in the wind. I think I mentioned I have Parkinson's. It makes me shake. How was this going to work?

I stood at the railing looking out over the incredible landscape and then down the side of the bridge. I was already shaking and couldn't imagine how I'd manage the small rungs of the ladder. Nonetheless, I swung a leg up and over the railing. Parkinson's or not, I was going over the side. I was going to complete this challenge.

Shaking like a leaf in the wind, I slowly made my way down the ladders and out onto the thin plank suspended in space. At what appeared to be hundreds of feet in the air, I needed to make my way out to the end of the plank, kneel down, retrieve my next clue (which was hanging from the bottom of the plank), and then jump off. Shuffling and shaking, I was sure I'd fall—but I managed to make my way to the end of the plank and pull up the next clue. The clue had somehow been suspended from the bottom of the plank and neatly tucked into a big Ziploc bag. It had a carabiner (spring clip) on it, which I attached to myself. Then, once the clue was secure, I stood up and jumped, screaming like a wild man, all the way down to the ravine floor (lowered safely by the harness and ropes).

Watching myself perform this task on television was so incredibly different from the actual experience. One, I didn't appear to be shaking at all, yet I'd felt as if I was about to rattle right off the plank. Weird. Two, I was moved by Tim Jr.'s pride in what the old man could still get done. With what I considered to be my first serious challenge of the race completed, the score stood at Tim one, Parkinson's none.

Our final clue of the leg said to head to Quails' Gate Winery and find Jon, the show's host, at the mat. We made a dash for the vehicle, leaving our soon-to-be nemeses on the bridge, whimpering from their fear of its height. (Eventually we became good friends with the sister team of Celina and Vanessa, but we did not start off on the best of terms.)

At Quails' Gate we arrived alone and then met Jon on the first mat of the race. We were thrilled not to be last, but then sorely disappointed when we were given a thirty-minute penalty for taking only one clue from the butterflies rather than the two that the first clue had instructed. That penalty cost us fifth place and the indignity of being referred to as "suckers" by Celina when they arrived to take our fifth-place spot.

We ended the day in sixth place out of nine. And when we finished the leg only a few minutes behind the Girls, we not only felt confident but also had a wee bit of knowledge. You see, early on we'd noticed the rising sun of the British Columbia flag on the first clue. We'd also spotted the B.C. dogwood flower on the lapel of the greeter who stood with Jon on the mat. Both of these tidbits would have a significant impact as the race unfolded.

Despite managing to get our first couple of mistakes under our belt, we weren't the first team eliminated on the first leg of the first season of *The Amazing Race Canada*. Thus, I was able to preserve my twins' mental well-being. I also had the opportunity to face the effects of my Parkinson's early on, and it went not too badly. We had an alarm clock, Cogsworth II, and we were on to leg two.

Leg one had given us our first glimpse of the difficulties we'd have and the responses we'd need to learn. The frustration of losing our only timepiece did lead to a certain creativity in solving the problem. But making a wrong turn that brought us in last to the butterfly conservatory and our error in taking only one clue were the first of many mistakes that would eat away at our confidence. Still, how the stress of the race would affect my Parkinson's had of course been a concern, so walking the plank in Kelowna was a great chance to experience the shaking it produced and see that I could handle it.

Although we'd made it through leg one, looking back, I wish we'd been able to acknowledge the stress and come to terms with it sooner. Instead, these events marked the beginning of a mountain of anxiety that would all but explode in leg three. Things had turned out all right, but the only lesson to be learned from leg one was that I didn't learn my lessons quickly enough.

chapter 8

How's Your Mandarin?

ONE OF THE THINGS I LOVE MOST about Canada is its vast diversity. There's something uniquely wonderful in our country's open-arms acceptance of multiple backgrounds. I so appreciate the fact that we can come from many different places, speak many different languages, and yet be completely Canadian. We experienced this firsthand in Vancouver's Chinatown.

The morning of leg two started as most of my days do: I crawled out of bed and began my stretching and yoga routine, one of the cornerstones in my fight against Parkinson's. The stretching and strength training ensures that I maintain the muscle tone, flexibility, and balance needed as this disease progresses.

Our first accomplishment of the day was to exact a bit of revenge on sisters Celina and Vanessa. So as Tim Jr. and I headed off in the SkyTrain to the Richmond Oval for our first task, we felt giddy—we'd left the Girls standing on the platform, having just missed the train. Then Tim Jr. knocked out the speed-skating task, circling the ice oval three times on his first try and in only forty of the ninety seconds he'd been given to complete it.

Next, we made our way to Chinatown, where we had a choice of two tasks. We opted for the more physical one: find six pieces of a lion costume and then perform a traditional Chinese dance. Our clue provided us with a list of locations where we'd find the pieces, except that it was in Mandarin— those unique characters that nigh on a billion people read but that might as well be Rorschach inkblots to me. This will likely come as no surprise to you, but the Tims were in shock to discover that everything in Chinatown was written in Chinese. I mentioned earlier that I hadn't traveled much around Canada before, and I guess I just assumed it would be similar everywhere. I mean, it's *Canada*.

Having become lost in translation, we began to despair. We found a number of people who could speak English but not quite enough Mandarin to interpret the list, along with what felt like hundreds of people who spoke Mandarin but not quite enough English. One woman was so eager to help that she'd watch for us every time we came by her store. Had we found the clues? she would ask in broken English. The answer was always no. She'd scold us in Mandarin while pointing in multiple directions and then send us on our way again.

Tim Jr. and I chased around Chinatown for over two hours. In time we came to realize that we were truly in another world: a community within a community that lived, worked, and celebrated life in another language. We might have been lost and confused, but the people here were very much at home. Many of them took great pleasure in watching us struggle, which was okay. What had seemed so out of place was indeed the norm; we were the ones out of place.

Finally, we came to the conclusion that we had to switch tasks. We were simply not getting this done: we'd found five of the six pieces we needed but just couldn't cross that last, final hurdle. We later discovered that many of the other teams had the same result and in the end switched as well. As much as we enjoyed the experience of the culture and the great amusement we provided the community, without that one person who could show us the way, we'd never make it. So we turned to the second task, which proved to be a smart decision.

This task involved finding a tea store, which we did relatively quickly, and having a cup of tea. Once we finished it, we turned the tea cup over to discover a Mandarin character. Then, having memorized it, we were to head to another location to reproduce it. This we accomplished with relative ease, releasing us from Chinatown.

Our new clue instructed us to head to the shipyards. After we'd made our way down to the water's edge, we found that we needed to climb a gigantic crane, one of those beasts that load cargo ships with containers. I have no idea how many stairs we climbed and descended that day, but it felt like billions. What made matters most fun was the fact that the stairs were antislip, meaning that below each step was what looked like a little explosion having gone off. Those jagged protrusions pointing skyward kept me from slipping, but too well—I could barely move my feet. With Parkinson's I often struggle to lift my left foot, and that antislip surface made life terrible.

Once we got to the top of the crane we needed to locate our next destination somewhere in the harbor with a pair of binoculars. Really? The only binoculars I've ever used were at the lake, where I'd occasionally watch squirrels and bald eagles. Jody, on the other hand, had his training as a sniper in the Canadian military to call on. He and Cory just happened to arrive right behind us. They (and by "they" I mean Jody) picked up the binoculars, found the location, and left. Yes, just that quickly. Fortunately, I had Tim Jr. He scanned the harbor, and not ten minutes later we were on our way to the grass-covered roof of the convention center.

Making my way down the crane's stairs was even worse than going up. I had to consciously think about each step I took, making sure that the toe of my left boot completely disengaged from the antislip protrusions. Even then I'd trip and stumble every few steps. The next time you're out for a walk, try to consciously think about every step you take. Every single one. While descending a billion stairs hundreds of feet in the air. That's what it felt like, and the prospect of falling was making me crazy. Anyway, when I finally made it to the bottom, we threw ourselves into our waiting cab and headed for the convention center.

So much of the race was a blur of excitement and confusion. And that day was no different: my mind was a whirlwind as we arrived at the convention center. Now, this was a massive facility, and of course we had no idea where to go. But as we jumped out of the cab and ran for the building, we noted two things. One, Dave and Jet (of the Brawn 1 team) were arriving at the same time: it would be a sprint for the mat. Two, Brett, from the Doctors team, was casually sitting on a step out front. Dave and Jet took off toward the other end of the building. Brett didn't move. He didn't speak. He merely looked to his right. And on his right was a door with a race flag on it. Had he just helped us?

We tore through the door and into the lobby. Nothing. We must need to go upstairs—so off to the escalators we went. They weren't working, though, so we had to climb two stories. Once again I was climbing stairs that were difficult to move my feet on, and all the while I was thinking, "Of course, why would the escalators work for the guy with Parkinson's?" Still, we made it to the roof and the mat well ahead of Dave and Jet. We were met by the show's host, Jon, and a gentleman from the Squamish Nation who had a white dogwood flower on his lapel. We'd started the day in sixth position, and we ended the day in sixth position. We had survived leg two.

For me, that leg featured a parallel to my journey with Parkinson's. I consider myself extraordinarily fortunate to have a nursing background while facing this disease. But even so, I often find myself just as lost in translation as I did in Chinatown. When I was diagnosed with Parkinson's at forty-six I knew no one my age who had the disease, since, as I've mentioned, the average age of onset is past sixty. So I felt as if I'd been thrust into a community where I knew little of its language and nothing of its people.

As a nurse, I had the ability to delve into the research and come away with a technical understanding of what was happening to my body. But just as in learning a language, true understanding involves much more than a technical reproduction of words. There's a context to language that can be found only in community. Deeper meaning, support, and understanding will come only as one learns the broader significance of what it means to live in a particular language or group. You first need friends who are like you, and early on I had none.

It's easy to understand how someone can become isolated in a new community in which they speak little of the language, where they have no friends and no supports. Now imagine this in a community that deals with an ailment they find embarrassing: the tremor that is ever present, the rigidity and slowness of gait, let alone the freezing that occurs when an individual simply cannot move. They get "stuck" as they try to walk. For these reasons and many more, people with Parkinson's tend to pull away and stay in the shadows.

There are many around the globe who are reaching out to the Parkinson's community. Organizations like the Michael J. Fox Foundation are working tirelessly to find a cure for Parkinson's. For this I am eternally grateful. However, I continually sense a need for a greater emphasis on wellness within the community while we await a cure. Far too often I meet those who seem to sit back and do little in hopes that a cure will come along to make everything better. I don't mean to be a pessimist, but I often ask people to name the last illness we've actually cured. The unfortunate reality is that we don't cure much.

We can, however, learn to live well with this disease: to learn its language, its rhythms, its community, and to thrive despite its reality (or that of any other ailment). I take great joy in being able to bridge some of these moments for people who have Parkinson's themselves or have loved ones with it. For the nurse in me, it's always heartening when I'm able to help people better understand what's happening to them and discover the things they can do to live better with the disease. This is a constant theme as I travel and encourage my audiences to *Live Your Best!* And it was the impetus behind founding my charity, U-Turn Parkinson's.

I urge people living with Parkinson's to engage with and build a personal community: a group of like-minded individuals who face the same struggles, seek the same answers, and are able to offer mutual assistance. Whether it's a support group, a Rock Steady Boxing club like the one I attend, or any other exercise group, these are people who understand what we're going through and can help us just as we can help them. Whether it's Parkinson's or any other challenge, one of the keys to living your best is realizing that you can't beat this thing alone—success can be had only in community.

It will remain my goal in life to be one of the healthiest people in line waiting for the cure when it arrives. I won't sit back and allow Parkinson's to destroy my world. I'll learn the language, understand the context of my new reality, and then encourage others to thrive with me in this battle. After all, unlike that first Chinatown challenge, I don't have the option here of switching tasks.

In Chinatown, the feeling of being totally lost and overwhelmed in a new environment was familiar to me, but we were fortunate enough to find a way through it. Yet we still had something to learn about paying attention to detail. Our clock, Cogsworth II, had a night-light function that was activated by releasing a little button at the bottom. Of course, while Cogsworth was traveling around in my backpack, that button had been on the whole time. Now the batteries were dead. Once again we were without a timepiece—an additional self-induced stress that was absolutely maddening. But this stress would prove to be mild compared with that brought on by the world's most complicated line dance.

chapter 9

This
Ain't No
Boot
Scootin'
Boogie

WE STARTED LEG THREE IN SIXTH POSITION, which doesn't sound all that bad until you understand the reality of the situation. At the end of leg one we'd been sixth of nine teams, and at the end of leg two, when we watched the Cowboys get eliminated, we were sixth of eight teams. The fact was that the cliff was crumbling behind us, and we needed to move up before we fell off.

Our next destination was the province of Alberta and the city of Calgary. On arrival, our clue directed us to the Ranchman's saloon and hinted at a line dance, which I thought was great news. Soon after Sheryl and I moved to Winnipeg we were down at the Forks, one of the loveliest outdoor spaces in the Peg, where I got into a little line dancing competition. I ended up the winner by doing something called the Boot Scootin' Boogie. I think it had more to do with my enthusiasm than my skill, but in any case I took home two tickets to a Blue Bombers CFL football game that day.

So my mind flashed back to days of glory. I was sure I could knock this challenge out and move us ahead of some of the other teams. Why oh why did we not remember that I now had Parkinson's, which has you beating a rhythm to your own drum and no one else's? That day I just could not keep time, nor could I figure out the very complex line dance we had to perform.

I'll be forever grateful to Dr. Holly, who took a bit of time to teach me some of the steps. Truth be told, without her help I may never have gotten any of that dance. I was shaking, completely off beat, and totally freaked out. After nine attempts, and by then so far behind the other racers that it couldn't possibly matter, the judges let me go. I feel compelled to apologize to the team of dancers I kept there, who repeated that dance every few minutes for well beyond three hours. They were incredibly patient, and I'm very grateful to them. At long last my humiliation was over (except for the later airing of it on national TV).

Tim Jr., ever the encourager, cheered wildly for me when I finally "completed" the challenge. I was feeling terrible about having delayed us so badly, but he fortified my spirits by pointing out that I hadn't given up and that we could now move on.

The next clue instructed us to drive ourselves in the provided Chevrolet pickup truck to the hoodoos. For the love of Pete, what is a "hoodoo"? We stopped at a gas station for a map, and what little information we could find told us that hoodoos are impressive rock formations created over the centuries by rain and wind. Our information also seemed to direct us toward a little town an hour and a half from Calgary called Drumheller. Panic, fear, frustration, anxiety, and any number of other feelings began to well up inside us. Finally, having made some further stops to ask questions and get directions, we set off for the town. It seemed like the right thing to do. Whether one or the other of us would have an aneurysm on that hour-and-a-half drive was yet to be seen. This could turn out to be a three-hour mistake.

After one of the longest drives of my life we arrived in Drumheller and, to our great relief, discovered the hoodoos. We climbed up into the hills to locate our next clue, which pointed the way to our next task: either shoveling coal or recreating a replica dinosaur. (Drumheller is famous for the dinosaur fossils that have been discovered in the area.) Figuring we didn't need another complicated challenge, Tim Jr. and I chose the coal.

We made our way into an old coal mine where we donned overalls, boots, gloves, and face masks. Back out in the heat of the day, we were directed to several mounds of coal and a number of waiting train cars. Most of the cars were already filled, leaving us the empties, which were farthest from the piles of coal. The task was to move the coal from the piles and fill our car until it passed inspection. After being given shovels and a wheelbarrow, we set to work.

What took the other teams an hour and a half or more to do, the Tims did in forty minutes. We crushed it! Tim Jr. came up with the brilliant idea of simply lifting and dumping our wheelbarrow into the train car instead of shoveling the coal back out of it. That saved us tons of time. I hate to admit it, but the complicated tasks were not our strong suit; the physical challenges, on the other hand, we could blow right through (as long as dancing wasn't involved). As counter-intuitive as it may sound for a guy with Parkinson's, we found that our strengths lay in the straightforward physical tasks. It turned out that we're fairly linear thinkers and don't do as well with the abstract. Thus, for the remainder of the race, we stuck to the physical tasks as much as possible.

Brawn versus brains? Maybe, but that's what worked for us. We chose to accept who we are and to play to our strengths—which is a profound lesson if we can learn it in life. At times it's been difficult for me to accept that I can't necessarily do everything I set my hand to. But Parkinson's has taught me that I have no choice but to simplify my focus. It's often not obvious how important this idea is: doing less so that you can do or be more.

In this way I've learned to exert a measure of control over my life that I hadn't thought possible. With the Parkinson's diagnosis came the sense that life was completely out of control—that I'd steadily lose abilities until I was bedridden or dead. Not true. Although this disease hinders my life, has cost me my job, and prevents me from doing many other things I might like to do, it continues to give to me in bafflingly good ways. My involvement as an advocate for Parkinson's, the speaking opportunities, and the work I do with our U-Turn Parkinson's charity in Winnipeg are all examples of the control I've gained even when I've lost control of other things.

Parkinson's hasn't simply taken from my life and left me barren. It has taken, it has caused great pain, but it's also given me the opportunity to grow through these seasons of pain into someone new, with new desires, new goals, and a greater aware-ness of pieces of me that I didn't know existed. It has taught me a new strength and a new patience, all the while showing me how much further I have yet to go as a human. I'm learning.

At the end of the coal challenge the train conductor handed us our next clue, which told us to find Jon at the mat. We were at the back of the pack, but determined that we wouldn't be sent home that day. We were hot and sweaty and full of confidence.

Then we got lost.

During our drive among the hoodoos we'd become increasingly convinced that we didn't know where we were going. As we were discussing our options—which, there in the middle of what felt like a desert, were few—an RCMP cruiser came into view behind us. I let him catch up, stuck my hand out the window, and started waving. In short, I did what anyone lost and on *The Amazing Race Canada* would do: I pulled over the cops. He gave us directions, and our hearts sank.

In recent years I've had the opportunity to go back to Drumheller to speak, and it's noteworthy that as you come into town there are three huge signs directing tourists to Horseshoe Canyon. But to find Jon at the mat, we needed to drive ourselves to Horsethief Canyon overlook. Tim Jr. was certain he'd seen it earlier in the day, except that he hadn't: he'd seen Horseshoe Canyon. And now we'd driven several minutes in the wrong direction. A few minutes may not seem like much, but things were that close. At the coal challenge Celina and Vanessa had told us who they'd seen— and it looked very likely that we'd be last. Our disappointment hung in the truck like the gloom of those being sent to the gallows. We were sure we'd sealed our fate.

Now that we were on the right track, we started to do the math. There wasn't much hope, but there was the small chance that this could be a non-elimination leg. Typically, when you come in last on a leg you're sent home; however, there are generally at least a couple of non-elimination legs where the team in last place is spared. What we didn't know was exactly how many legs were planned, and so by our estimation the "non-elim," as they came to be called, could easily come in either leg three or four. In short, we had no better than a fifty-fifty chance of being saved. I felt physically sick at the thought of being sent home so early in the race, not to mention the prospect of embarrassing my family.

It was a bright, beautiful day in Alberta and there was Jon, standing on the mat at the edge of Horsethief Canyon over-look, which at least provided a fantastic view as a backdrop for our anxiety. Once we reached the mat, Jon—along with a cowboy in a white hat, brown vest, brown chaps, and a wild rose on his lapel—greeted us. Then we heard those fateful words that every team dreads: "Boys, you're the last team to arrive." I can tell you exactly what was going through my mind just then. I was hot, disappointed, embarrassed, and oh so not ready to leave this incredible adventure. But then Jon got this little look on his face and said, "However . . ." The word "however" will forevermore be among my most favorite in the English language. "However," he said, "this is a non-elimination leg and you boys are still in this race!"

I was thrilled; my heart soared. In the very next instant, though, it sank. Embarrassment had been averted, the elimi-nation bullet dodged, we weren't going home—but there was a small problem: *we weren't going home*. In that moment an internal battle was going on—one part of me was so grateful to avoid elimination and the other part just wanted this whole thing to be over. I wasn't sleeping well, I wasn't eating well, I was tired of fighting with my Parkinson's, and I hadn't spoken to my wife since leaving home (calls home weren't allowed). We couldn't seem to figure out the rhythm of this race. A small part of me just did not want it to continue.

This moment in the race so closely parallels my struggle with Parkinson's that it's unnerving. In many ways, I'm one of the healthiest people I know with the disease. And although it's brought more good into my life than bad, it remains a relentless "race" that I seldom seem able to fully grasp. There are, of course, times when I wish Parkinson's would just stop. That I could go back home and get on with my life. I get so very tired of this race that I'm clearly not going to win.

At this point in *The Amazing Race* we had little reason to believe that success could ever be realized. We were lucky to have come last on a non-elim, but it still meant a penalty the next day: not only would we start in last place but we'd have an additional task to complete as well. Most people watching this part later on TV understood that there wasn't much chance of our surviving. And just as hope began seeping away from those who followed us on the race, hope can be an elusive friend in life. After all, living with Parkinson's is much like having an extra task every day. I can't change the outcome of the course I'm on, so why would I even try? This is the sentiment to which we can easily succumb.

I see many with Parkinson's who simply give up, and at some level, how can you blame them? No matter how hard we struggle, the brute facts remain. How do you keep moving forward when everything points to the reality that you're going to lose? I had dreams and aspirations for my life that did not include Parkinson's. I hadn't imagined that life, or the race, would go this way.

Yet here we were, stuck in what appeared to be a never-ending spiral into oblivion and humiliation. It was only a matter of time until we'd complete our folly in front of the nation. The cliff was eroding away behind us. Parkinson's, too, will slowly consume my world and leave me helpless. What I sometimes wish for—that it would all just go away—is what I'll never get. So as I stood there on the mat that day with Tim Jr., Jon, and a cowboy, a part of me truly did just want to go home.

Brett and Holly (the Doctors) had barely beaten us to the mat. "Not being a physical team," as the pair noted so many times throughout the race, they'd chosen to construct a dinosaur skeleton, which had turned out to be extremely difficult. So they'd come to the mat with the same trepidation we had, except that their day ended in gleeful disbelief: they'd finished ahead of us. Had I done one less twirl on the dance floor or had we not gotten lost (map-reading lessons next time maybe?), we wouldn't have ended the day in last place.

However (still love that word), we were still in the race. Tim Jr. and I headed back to our dinosaur-inspired hotel, the surrounding badlands so full of bones and hoodoos that the place seemed like a replica of the Flintstones' town of Bedrock. And as we sat together that evening, there was only one question on our minds: "How in the world are we going to turn this around?"

I'm not sure how, but at one point we began to discuss

Tim Jr.'s tattoos. I'm not much of a tattoo guy, but of my four children, the two eldest all but came out of the womb saying, "Daddy, can I have a tattoo?"

Daddy has always said no. I've told them that on their eighteenth birthday they can put on their bodies whatever they choose, but not before. Each, on their eighteenth birthday, got a tattoo. What can I say? A parent can only try.

Still, I have little room to complain about either of Tim Jr.'s tattoos. On his left inner bicep he has the symbol of the Trinity, and on his back is a two-word reference to Psalm 46:10: "Cease striving."

We began to discuss the meaning of the word "strive." If you look it up you'll find that it comes from the old English for "to contend, to quarrel, to fight" as well as the old French for "strife." It carries with it a burden of anxiety—that freaked-out, stressed-out way of thinking that says, "By god, I'm going to make this happen no matter what it takes!"

We realized that we'd come into the race with an attitude of striving—we were going to do whatever it took to win, we were going to make it happen—and that it wasn't working for us. We also realized that we weren't having any fun.

How on earth could we be here and not be having a good time? We'd beaten out ten thousand other teams who'd love to be in our place—even in last place—on this incredible journey. How could we miss enjoying the ride?

We made a decision that evening to start having fun. We also decided to get up every morning during the race and just do our best. We wanted to let go of this insane, stressed-out mindset we'd gotten ourselves into. We would relax.

Maybe you're thinking that this is the kind of thing losers

say after they've lost the race. It sounds trite, simplistic, even a little silly: *The Tims made it onto national television but they couldn't get their act together and really sucked. So they decided to start having fun and do their best* . . . Yeah, I know.

As I travel and share my story, I'm always worried that I'll lose my listeners at this point. But bear with me. This is where I'm reminded of that old proverb, "All you really need to know you learned in kindergarten."

My kindergarten teacher, you might remember, was Mrs. Popovich. Throughout my kindergarten career Mrs. Popovich and I would start off almost every day the same way. I'd come into the classroom and she'd look at me and say, "Timmy, shut up!" For you see, I never had any problem talking. That might be a mild overstatement. But more importantly, she would often say to me, "Timmy, just do your best."

It was good advice. We live in a culture that continually tells us that who we are and what we do and have is not good enough. We are exhorted to have more, to be more, to show up and give a hundred and ten percent every day. But that's an impossibility. The best we can ever give is our best.

When I speak to corporate audiences across North America, I'll often ask, "Who here can give a hundred and ten percent to your job today?" Invariably a few hands will go up. But no matter how well-meaning we are, it's just not true that any of us can give more than a hundred percent.

There are days when I get up and my Parkinson's won't allow me to function as I can on better days. There are good days when I basically feel normal and can do practically anything I want. The fact is, I can't alter what my best will look like from day to day. Neither can you. There are things that will occur today that will alter your performance and you'll have no say in the matter.

Then there are the days when I'm plain lazy, but of course that's another issue altogether. The only thing I have a choice in is how I'm going to respond to my circumstances on any given day—and that choice is about deciding to give my best. Not some mystical hundred and ten percent that no one can attain.

I'll never forget the day I sat in my neurologist's office and discussed with him the mind-numbing fatigue I'd been experiencing. I had no energy. I'd always been the kind of guy who could handle a full-time job along with doing a part-time job on the side, running marathons, cycling to work, looking after the family, and still having a bit of juice left over. Now I was barely getting through work.

My doctor had the audacity to suggest that I'd have to "choose" what I wanted to do and start letting other things go.

Right in front of the doc and my wife, I started to cry. I was embarrassed, and so angry I could barely contain myself. My soul ached—I felt I was being talked to as though I were eighty. Who did this guy think he was to tell me I couldn't do what I wanted to do? I was forty-nine years old and by god I was going to make this happen. No one and no illness was going to tell me what I could or could not do.

The nurse in me knew better, but I was determined to prove that I could do this thing. Parkinson's wasn't going to define my life; *I'd* be the one to set the parameters on what would and wouldn't be.

In other words, I was striving with my Parkinson's, just as

Tim Jr. and I had been striving up to that point in the race. But I came to see that I needed to be able to accept what my best is on a day-to-day basis, and to learn the strength I'd need to be content with what that best produces. Since then I've chosen to get up every day, have fun, and do my utmost. And that was what we determined to do as we continued in the race.

With our heads in a clearer place, Tim Jr. and I were still in need of finding replacement batteries for our alarm clock. What to do? We couldn't just go out and buy new ones. We'd need to be creative.

At breakfast the following morning we struck up a conversation with our waitress, Dani. She was a sweet, curious young lady. I need to point out here that at no time during the race could we divulge who we were or what we were up to. And although we certainly didn't divulge anything to Dani, it was pretty clear she had a hunch as to what was going on.

As we chatted, we mentioned our need of two batteries, casually wondering if she might discreetly help us obtain some. It was delightful to see the look on her face shift from confusion to excited "Aha!"

Then, just as quickly, her expression went blank and mysterious. She leaned in close and, with a convincing James Bond–like demeanor, said, "I'm on it."

A few minutes later she returned to ask how our meal had been. As she removed our plates she laid a fresh, green cloth napkin on the table.

". . . And here's a new napkin for you."

Not another word was exchanged, but inside the napkin were four brand-new batteries. As we walked out of the restaurant, my eyes met Dani's. My smile and nod of the head was reciprocated, sealing our moment of intrigue. We now had batteries for Cogsworth II, and the wisdom to take them out of the clock when packing it.

Our day in Drumheller had been an insightful one for Tim Jr. and me. We'd learned something about ourselves and the race, and felt prepared to move forward. So, given our newfound frame of mind and clearer sense of purpose, I wish I could tell you that the Tims' game play radically changed. It did not. We continued to suck.

chapter 10

Perseverance

PERSEVERANCE—that great big long word we don't use very much anymore. We don't seem to like it, I find, possibly because it's so often associated with bad things, struggles, and hardship. Coming out of Drumheller, Tim Jr. and I were full of hope that, as long as we remained positive, we could turn our game around. This wasn't the case: our positive thoughts produced precious little in results. It became clear that these thoughts weren't enough, that we'd need to work even harder to stay in the race. Yet despite our best efforts, leg after leg we continued to struggle. This is where we learned the meaning of the word "perseverance."

As we began to consider our experiences and the role perseverance played in them, we realized that Tim Jr. couldn't quite spell it at first and that I didn't remember exactly what it meant. So we turned to Google. If you look up the word, you'll find a definition something like this: *"to carry on in your course of action, even in the face of difficulty, with little or no evidence of success."* That definition should come with an image of the Tims' faces. At no time throughout the course of the race did we ever show any evidence that we'd be successful. This continued struggle could have been our undoing, but we chose to have hope.

Hope. An elusive commodity, something we all want and feel we need just to survive certain days. Yet all too often any hope we might possess gets slowly eroded by the constant drip of persistent struggle. There have been times in life when I've marveled at those around me for whom things always seem to go right. Those for whom life seems to deal only aces—and if they're dealt a joker it serves to turn their mish-mash of a hand into a flush.

Throughout the course of the race we were told many times how lucky we were. We were reminded over and over of how things kept falling our way. Only a few family members or friends pointed out our determination to persevere no matter what occurred. Some days I find it far too easy to look at others and think that life just treats them way nicer than it does me. I fail to realize that those who "get lucky" often do so because day after day they've chosen to get up, work hard, and persevere. As a former employer of mine used to say, "Eighty percent of success is just showing up every day."

When I'm asked where that will to persevere came from, I always answer the same way. It all goes back to that day in August 2010 when my big toe started twitching and then my subsequent diagnosis. After crashing and burning for about a year, as I talked about earlier, I knew there were only three ways to look at that diagnosis. First, I could try to ignore it, treat it as if it were benign and could be put on a shelf.

Well, I'd tried that, and it's just not possible. Parkinson's will not be ignored. My tremor is worse today than it was in August 2010, I have a stiffness that didn't exist then, and fatigue is much more of an issue now. The anxiety and depression that ultimately robbed me of my nursing career can only be ignored at my peril.

Second, I could raise a fist to heaven and scream, "Why me?" That wouldn't have surprised some. The urge to be angry with God was very real, but ultimately I knew it wasn't a balanced response. It didn't seem honest of me to blame God, or anyone else, when I so seldom gave thanks or credit for all the good that has come into my life. When you consider my life overall, how could I justifiably be angry? Having been rescued at birth and given a great set of parents and a home; having been born in North America and blessed with all its abundance; having been given good health for the first forty-six years of life, a great education, gainful and meaningful employment, a loving wife, four fabulous, healthy children, a daughter-in-law, a granddaughter, and *The Amazing Race Canada*—all this standing in one column beside Parkinson's in the other. I have far more to be thankful for than I have to be angry about. Needless to say, I abandoned the "curse God and die" option.

Now I may be a simple kind of guy, but in my mind's eye I had only one option left. If Parkinson's couldn't be ignored, and if I were to choose not to let it be a curse, I had to assume that it must be a blessing. That there had to be something in this thing that was good for both me and those around me. So from that day on I've chosen to embrace Parkinson's. It has become my new best friend whom I hate. (Whoever said you had to like every blessing?) I hope it's beginning to become clear that it's not necessarily the nice, easy things in life that bring the greatest benefits.

Just as I'd chosen to believe that Parkinson's couldn't have my life, during the race I decided that it couldn't take *The Amazing Race Canada* from me. I was determined to face every challenge with the very best of my ability, no matter what my best looked like—I would persevere through every task, every day, until all was left on the field. Either I'd prevail or I'd come up short. Only with this mindset could I be content if we were eliminated from the race.

The race has taught me that we can choose how we respond to hardship. An oak doesn't grow into a strong, majestic tree by being raised in a greenhouse. Once the seedling is mature it's planted out on the bald prairie of Manitoba. There it's rained on, snowed on, possibly hit by lightning. As it stands against the elements its roots go deep and it finds solid rock to hold on to. And as it finds footings below, up above its branches grow wide; they leaf and become shelter, shade, and protection for those around it. The same can be said for those of us living with Parkinson's or with any other such struggle. Unlike a tree, though, we can choose to embrace this time in our lives and be made stronger by it. It doesn't mean that our circumstances will get easier; in fact, they often become worse. However, we can be made better people because of these trials if we allow them to shape our character rather than crush our spirit. It's when we've come through hardship that we know hope best.

In Malcolm Gladwell's book *David and Goliath* he talks about the people of London during the Luftwaffe bombing in the Second World War. Gladwell describes the incredible transformation that occurred in some who survived the bombings day after day. They came *to expect to survive*. I love that. They took precautions to protect themselves, but they'd go about their daily lives as best they could, all the while growing less terrified of the daily bombardment.

This is the lesson I try to apply to my life with Parkinson's. Some days it may be terrible and I can anticipate that it will get worse. It will likely one day be debilitating and may even impact my death. However, today I'm very much alive and well. I'm learning to expect to survive each day, and more than that, to live to the best of my ability.

This may sound simple, but it's something I've had to learn. We have the option to embrace our suffering. I have no choice in the fact that I've been given Parkinson's. I do, however, have a choice in how I live with it. I can allow it to be a tremendous evil in my life or I can acknowledge that it's given me far more than it's taken.

As I've embraced this new best friend whom I hate, I've been taught perseverance. And along the way, just like that mighty oak, I have found my character deepened. Perseverance has worked in me a willingness to see life differently, to adjust my expectations and desires. I'm learning to be more patient with myself and my world.

Perseverance has also worked this mysterious concept of contentedness into my life. Rarely have I been able to sit still; I've often had to be reminded to slow down and smell the roses. To celebrate the victories in life rather than rushing on to the next endeavor. But if there's anything that Parkinson's produces in me, it's a desire to sit still. This tremor leaves me aching for times when my limbs are quiet—and when those moments do arrive, I'm filled with joy and peace. I've come to enjoy them so much that I seek out ways to create them. And in doing so I've discovered the quiet that's there waiting for us if only we slow down enough to experience it.

Parkinson's has led me to appreciate perseverance, a journey that is deepening and maturing my character, guiding me into a greater understanding of contentment. And, strangely enough, this deepening of character has taught me hope. I'm discovering that I *can* live with this disease. I'm still of value to those who love me. I can still dream dreams and anticipate that many of them will be fulfilled. I've seen that despite worsening symptoms, the need to leave my nursing career, and the need to give up some other things, too, there are many things I can do, and they bring meaning to my world. I can still live a life that brings meaning to others.

"Perseverance" often elicits difficult emotions. Yet it's a new friend whom I hold close—whom I have no choice but to hold close if I want to succeed in this race with Parkinson's.

*

We went into leg four feeling conflicted. We'd survived the non-elimination, but now we needed to complete an additional challenge. We were still in the race, but of course that meant I couldn't go home. Still, we got to have a bit of fun before the next challenges. Since none of the other teams knew about leg three being a non-elim, they'd be assuming we were out. It was time for a little surprise. Once we'd made our way to the airport for our flight to Yellowknife, Northwest

Territories, we walked into the waiting room—and just as we'd anticipated, our fellow contestants were all taken aback to see us, with more than a few looking unhappy. We enjoyed that.

Once in Yellowknife, we set off in search of a particular spot along the Great Slave Lake shoreline. Then, of course, we got lost. We went all over town (and the town was not that big) looking for the right dock. At last we found it, jumped out, and ran half a kilometer across the ice to our next challenge.

The task was for one of us to get into a swimsuit, jump into a hole cut in the ice, and retrieve our next clue. Fortunately we could choose who would take this one on. I hate being cold, and I'm not a big fan of water. So even before the race began we'd agreed that, when we had the choice, Tim Jr. would do any water challenges and I'd step up for anything to do with food.

Raring to go, Tim Jr. tore off to the swimming hole, where he was immediately strapped into a safety harness. But just as he went to jump in, a howl arose from Dave (of the Brawn 1 team), who complained that we'd cut in line. It made for a bit of drama, but we hadn't intentionally cut him off (not to suggest that I wouldn't have, given the chance); rather, Tim Jr. had simply done as he was instructed.

Nonetheless, we took our place behind Dave. Finally Tim Jr. plunged into the hole. In a frozen lake. In the Northwest Territories. Just thinking about it makes me shake! But he retrieved our clue, climbed up the ladder, and emerged in one piece.

Then (once he'd gotten into warm clothes) he led the way back to the car and off we went to the airport. There we needed to sign up, in order of arrival, for one of three waiting planes that would leave a full twenty minutes apart. We were fortunate to make the first plane. But Jody and Cory (Brawn 2) made the mistake of not paying attention when they signed up; they could have been on the second flight but instead ended up on the third, an oversight that almost cost them the leg. It was painful to watch them ask Hal and Jo (the BodyBreak duo) if they could have a place on the second plane—in vain, since no team would ever consider giving up a clear advantage.

We took off in a single-engine Otter—your classic bush plane—and went winging our way over some of Canada's most beautiful tundra. I love flying in these types of planes: you can hear the wind at the doors; you're low enough to truly enjoy the scenery; you actually *feel* like you're flying. What a great time that was.

Of all the visual gifts the race gave us, Carcross, Yukon, proved to be an unforgettable splendor. With its stunning tundra surrounded by white-capped peaks, the barrenness and wildness of the land was palpable. Then came the traversing of just a few short kilometers between a frozen lake and the world's smallest desert, complete with sand dunes—a beautifully contradictory experience.

Our first challenge in Carcross was the dreaded Speed Bump, or our extra task. We were in fairly good position, having gotten ourselves on the first plane, but we still needed to knock this one out fast. Our assignment was to perfectly memorize the first two stanzas of the Robert Service poem

"The Shooting of Dan McGrew." I was thrilled by the prospect, since I've always enjoyed, and been fairly good at, memorization. Tim Jr., however, did not share my enthusiasm.

We decided to split up the stanzas so that I'd have three segments and he'd have two. The first couple of tries were pretty rough. Tim Jr. was wound up and nervous, and we were close to losing it with each other. But when I realized that I was being a bit pushy, I tried to settle down; after that, we managed to keep our composure. It took a number of tries, but we got the job done and were able to move on. Now it was just a matter of how far back the Speed Bump had put us. We needed to catch up to the other teams.

As it turned out, we were okay, with a number of teams still working through either of the next two tasks: building a raft out of planks, rope, and fifty-gallon drums, or completing a maze with one person blindfolded and the other in a wheel-barrow. We opted for the latter.

Before we got to the maze, though, we had to slice off the end of a large tree by handling a two-man saw. Check. Next up was throwing a small hatchet and sticking it in a target. Tim Jr. nailed it on his first attempt. Evidently he hadn't inherited that skill from his dad—it took me five throws.

Then, as Tim Jr. slipped on blacked-out goggles, I got into an old wheelbarrow with a prospector's pan on my lap; the idea was to direct Tim Jr. through the maze as I picked up gold nuggets. Finally, once we'd collected them all, we were given our next clue: find Jon at the mat in the Carcross Desert.

Just as we were leaving we did a quick head count, since, unusually, we could see both tasks going on. Dave and Jet (Brawn 1), Hal and Jo, and the Docs had already left; the

Hippies, Kristen and Darren, were still building their raft; and Jody and Cory (Brawn 2) were just arriving. The Girls, Celina and Vanessa, had left a bit before us, having used their Express Pass, which allowed you to skip the task and go directly to the next. (The Hippies, who'd been awarded two passes for coming in first on a previous leg, had given one of them to the Girls, and we wondered why they hadn't used it themselves. They continued to work away even though it was now down to them and Brawn 2.)

Anyway, as long as nothing went wrong, we were looking to be in pretty good shape. With that we turned on our heels and got on our way to hunt for Jon.

We were shown to a set of quad bikes and then tore off through the desert/tundra/snow in search of the mat. It didn't take long until we were on foot again, running through the desert and over dunes. It was exhausting work. But finally, as we crested a ridge, our hearts soared. Not only was the mat in sight but Celina and Vanessa were running back toward us! It turns out that they'd dropped their packs too soon and had to retrieve them (teams weren't allowed to drop their packs in their rush to the mat until Jon could see them, and theirs had been left out of sight).

We raced to overtake them. Now, when I say "race" I mean I walked a little faster; no way my Parkinson's would let me run across the sand. But we moved as quickly as possible, and in the end came in mere seconds behind the Girls. Having started the day with that Speed Bump, we'd finished it fifth out of seven teams. We were absolutely thrilled.

Then, after waiting for the last two teams to arrive, we had the pleasure of watching a tremendous spectacle.

Jody, who'd lost both legs in Afghanistan and now walked on prosthetics, was understandably slower than most. Add to that the difficulty of running across the snow and sand, and odds were that Darren and Kristen would show up first. But to our amazement, it wasn't the Hippies who crested the dune next.

A guy with the spirit of a champion was running, yes, running across the desert on prosthetics. My jaw hit the ground at the sight of this man gutting out this task, destroying any perceptions that he was somehow disabled. It was a sight I doubt I'll ever forget. It brought a whole new level of respect for this competitor.

The last team to arrive would be the one bearing an Express Pass. Why the Hippies hadn't used it to keep them in the race still baffles me. Afterward they explained that they were excited about finishing the task. They did finish it, but it cost them the race. They were eliminated.

Four legs down and the Tims weren't looking great, but they were still in the game. Watching this leg of the race later on television, it felt somewhat anticlimactic. We seemed to just work through the day and then end it in fifth place. Nothing stellar. Nothing exciting. Until you remember that we'd come in last the day before. That had meant a huge burden of fear, not to mention being the only team with an extra task to perform. Yet despite all that, we were able to move up a spot in the standings.

Perseverance. It's not always sexy. It's not often exciting. And it can be lonely. What does it take to keep walking forward despite all the evidence that you're likely done? What does it take to keep moving when there's little chance you can improve your position and a likely chance that you'll be sent home? That day we proved that just showing up and continuing to work hard, regardless of what it looked like, was enough. Tomorrow would be another day.

We also did what we said we were going to do: we had a great time. When people ask what my favorite race destination was, I always put Carcross at the top of the list. We learned to enjoy and have fun with the race. We tackled the day to the best of our ability, and we were exceptionally content with the results.

Talk to me about Parkinson's. Tell me what I'm not supposed to be able to do. Tell me about all the limitations that will be placed on me and I'll tell you about a guy who beat Parkinson's on a snow-covered sand dune in Carcross, Yukon. I'll fight to prevent this disease from defining me, and I encourage you to live the same way. I can't get rid of my burden outright, but in Carcross I reminded it that it wasn't in charge.

As Tim Jr. and I drifted off to sleep that night, we felt relieved that the day had gone as well as it had and excited about starting the next leg. None of the teams knew the misery that awaited. Leg five would take us to Regina, Saskatchewan, home of the CFL Roughriders. For a Winnipeg boy, this would require a special kind of perseverance.

chapter 11

Death by Lentils

WE WERE NOW ENTERING what was essentially the halfway point in the race. We'd somehow made it this far. Once we arrived in Regina, we prepared ourselves for what would prove to be an epic day. It was a beautiful, sunny summer morning with temperatures near thirty degrees Celsius.

The first challenge was to locate a grain elevator out on the flat prairie. Having gotten lost only once, we finally found it. Adjacent to the elevator were a number of semitrailers, each filled with lentils. This episode was dubbed "Death by Lentils," and with good reason.

Our task was to climb into the back of a trailer and search for two small stuffed moose, each about four inches tall. Attached to each moose was a partial clue to our next destination. We were required to have both before we could move on.

The next time you're on the road and pull up alongside a semitrailer, take a good look at how big they really are. They're massive. Now imagine yourself inside that trailer swimming in a sea of lentils five or six feet deep, under a clear blue sky and a sweltering sun. We'd been thrown into a vegetable stew, and we were the beef stock.

With us at the task were Brett and Holly (the Doctors), Celina and Vanessa, and Hal and Joanne (of BodyBreak). We each had a semitrailer to ourselves and were stewing away in the heat. Tim Jr. and I decided to divide our trailer into sections and work together on one section at a time, making sure to dig deep into each. To our amazement, within about twenty minutes we had our first clue! We were crazy with excitement, but we kept this little discovery to ourselves and kept working.

At some point I thought I'd see how the others were doing. When we'd arrived, Hal and Jo, along with the Docs, had already been at it for at least an hour, and I was curious about their success so far, or lack thereof. When I popped my head over the side of our trailer, right away I could tell that neither team had yet found a clue. Hal had emerged for a moment just then, and what I saw both worried me and filled me with hope.

The nurse inside me was concerned that he looked so completely haggard. Sweat poured down his face, lentils dotted his head and arms, and his eyes were wide and desperate. On the other hand, as he withdrew into his trailer without seeing me, I began to think we might just have a chance. Hal and Jo were a tough team; they'd never been out of the top four. We already had one clue. We needed only to find the second.

There had been an ongoing conversation between the Docs and BodyBreak about taking a penalty just to free themselves from the pressure cookers they'd found themselves in. (Teams had the option of skipping a task and incurring an unknown time penalty—anywhere from thirty minutes to two hours.) At one point Brett called over to ask if we were interested in joining them. But with half the clue already in hand, we were in no mood to incur a penalty. We just wanted to finish, get out, and get a lead on the others.

So we settled back into our personal stewpot and continued our furious search. Then, once more to our amazement, we found the other half of the clue. While the others had been at the task for over two hours, it had taken us a mere forty minutes. Lady luck had shone on us again! As we ran for our vehicle I looked back to see both teams climbing out of their trailers. They were going to take the penalty. Two of the strongest teams on the race, BodyBreak and the Docs, were having a seriously bad day.

Our miniature moose held clues that directed us to the Royal Canadian Mounted Police training grounds. Once there, one member of each team had to make up a cadet's quarters to exacting standards. We decided that I'd take on the challenge. Then some good news: the first to have arrived, Jet and Dave, were still working on their room. Tim Jr. and I suddenly found ourselves in the running for first place.

Then Joanne showed up. While I struggled with the RCMP uniform, along with its "congress" boots and stirrups, she flew through the challenge. So much for staying ahead. It was an incredibly frustrating assignment that required an intense attention to detail. Shirts had to be hung and buttoned just so. Pants had to be suspended from their hanger through the zipper and the zipper zipped up. The boots required stirrups, which had an up side and a down side and which had to be put on with leather straps, which had a specific over-and-under order. Those stirrups just about cost me my sanity, but with some patience I was able to figure them out. However, we were now well behind Dave and Jet and Hal and Joanne.

With the cadet room made up to specifications, we were off to Mosaic Stadium, home of the Saskatchewan Roughriders (and the archrivals of the Winnipeg Blue Bombers). On our arrival, we were thrilled to discover that the Doctors and Hal and Jo were still there. Both teams were struggling mightily to complete their tasks: a cheerleading routine (the Docs) and football drills (Hal and Jo). You can guess which task Tim Jr. and I chose.

Kahari Jones, the one-time quarterback for the Winnipeg Blue Bombers, had traded in the blue and gold for Roughrider green and was now our "coach." He put us through our drills, and, being reasonably athletic, we were able to sail through them in two attempts: after running a lap around Mosaic Stadium, I played wide receiver and caught a pass from Tim Jr., who proceeded to put one through the uprights for an extra point, sealing our completion of the challenge. It was all such incredible fun. The only thing that could have made the whole thing better would have been to perform it in Winnipeg.

Next we were instructed to head to the press box high up on the opposite side of the field. Hot, sweaty, exhausted, and itchy (from wearing Rider green), we made our way up the innumerable steps to discover the Double U-Turn sign. (A U-Turn is an opportunity to force another team to complete an extra task in that leg—slowing them down and possibly even eliminating them from the race.) Our chance had arrived. Dave and Jet had come and gone long before, but the Docs and Hal and Jo were still struggling down on the field.

Tim Jr. wasn't too sure about U-Turning anyone, since it does pose a risk—it will undoubtedly make you a bad guy, which could come back to bite you if someone later gets the chance to do the same to you. I, on the other hand, had no qualms whatsoever. In my mind, this was a game we'd come to do our very best to win. I saw an opportunity to use a legitimate part of the game to push our fortunes forward.

We had an alliance with Brett and Holly, so they were safe. We'd really come to enjoy our friendship with the Docs, and after they'd helped us in Calgary with the line dance we'd agreed to protect one another when we could. Plus, although the Docs are brilliant people, they weren't so great at the more physical challenges. It was Hal and Jo who were the greater threat overall: they could perform physically and were continually in the lead. There was no doubt in my mind who we needed to U-Turn. The BodyBreakers were just too strong a team not to take a shot at.

Like us, they'd chosen to do the football drills as their first task. It took a number of tries, but they got it done. And because they completed it at the same time as the Docs, they found themselves in a foot race to the press box. It was clear that Hal was anticipating a U-Turn opportunity: on the show you can hear him encouraging Jo up the stairs with the admonition that they needed to U-Turn the Docs.

So once they reached the press box, they were mystified to discover that they themselves had been U-Turned. (They were also looking pretty tired—those two-plus hours in the lentils had clearly taken their toll.) Hal and Jo now had to return to the football field and perform a cheerleading routine before they could move on. It also became imperative that they U-Turn the Docs (that's where the "Double" U-Turn comes in), who'd have to perform the football drills. Hal and Jo would have no chance of survival otherwise.

Both teams now engaged in an epic battle on the sports field—a physical challenge that resulted in a blinding victory over Canada's fitness gurus by two self-professed nonathletes. Brett, who'd never kicked a football in his life, hit a field goal on his first try. And Holly, who'd never been known to catch a football, caught a pass on her first try. Brains had won out over brawn, and BodyBreak was left broken.

At the end of the day we came in second, just behind Dave and Jet. We helped save our friends the Docs and we still had our alarm clock, Cogsworth II. And while I'm still not much of a Roughrider fan, Regina will forever hold a warm spot in my heart.

Many people who later watched the show felt that the use of the U-Turn was mean-spirited. But it's one of the game's features, and was deployed within the rules. We took the opportunity to slow another team and try to advance our standing. And in the end, it did help our cause. If the goal is to win, then it was clearly the right choice to make. So why am I about to spend so much time discussing the U-Turn and what it represents? Because part of my Live Your Best credo is a willingness to use the openings that come your way.

The opportunities that enter our lives shouldn't be thrown off just because we're uncomfortable with them or afraid of what others might think. Take yoga. A lot of guys I know refuse to do it, even though it's been a huge help to me. Parkinson's leads to stiffness and decreased mobility. Yoga helps with the stiffness, which helps me move better. Yet when I tell this to the guys, some of them look at me as if I should be committed. We need to recognize that our biases sometimes prevent us from taking advantage of opportunities that may very well be good for us. There are times when we need to set those biases aside and act on what information we're given.

This is another aspect of what it means to persevere: having the guts to take an uncomfortable route or make a decision that others may disagree with. You take the opportunity not with the goal of hurting someone else but in hopes of enhancing your well-being.

In our "race" with Parkinson's, we also aim to win—to help slow its progression and, ultimately, to eliminate it. This is why we've named our charity in Winnipeg "U-Turn Parkinson's." *The Amazing Race* inspired me in many ways, but we've borrowed this one concept from the race and apply it to all we do in helping people live their best despite having the disease.

Our intention is to offer opportunities for those physical activities that have been shown to be of significant benefit in easing the symptoms of Parkinson's, and that in turn have a positive impact on emotional well-being. UTP also offers services that provide for the social needs of individuals; that is, the opportunity to hang out with those in similar circumstances.

And we work to help people living with Parkinson's lead fuller lives, whether that's in an intellectual, spiritual, or occupational way. All with the intent of slowing the progression of the disease, mitigating the damage it can do in each of these spheres, and ultimately eliminating the damage altogether.

Individuals with Parkinson's so often find themselves adrift in a sea of despair, unable to find the clues that will take them to a better place. So it's my desire to work with others in providing the help and encouragement people need, not only to survive this disease but also to thrive in spite of it. I've said it before: that means having the strength to do our best, the courage to be content with what our best produces, and the will to persevere. We know that in life we can get lucky, but to succeed we must be willing to take advantage of whatever opportunities we're given. And we'll take every opportunity to U-Turn Parkinson's.

chapter 12

Regard
dans
les Canons

WE CAME OUT OF LEG FIVE riding high off our U-Turn—
the first to have been used in the race. From Regina we
were on our way to Quebec City, and I was incredibly happy
about that. I'd never been east of Toronto, let alone visited
la belle province. We were also beginning to come into our
own, to better understand the rhythms of the race, although
it continued to be a roller coaster.

Dave and Jet were able to get the last seats on the earliest
flight out of Regina. We were on the second flight, which
had a layover in Toronto, and as soon as we landed there the
other teams on our flight headed off to see whether they
could secure earlier connections. The Tims? Oh, we went
for coffee. Some days I'm baffled by my own incompetence.

That lack of foresight (once we realized it) stressed us
out. But again we were lucky—our little coffee break didn't
harm our standing, although we wouldn't know it until later
in the day.

Having landed in Quebec City that evening, we were instructed to make our way to the Lévis Forts, which had been built to protect Canada from American invasion. I had to chuckle at this bit of irony. It was well after dark when Tim Jr. and I arrived at this historical site, but to our utter delight we found it closed and all the teams ahead of us present and accounted for. It looked like the race wouldn't continue until the next morning.

Yet there was a heavy sense of expectation in the air. The other teams seemed jittery. So, just to be safe, we decided to search the fort to make sure we wouldn't miss any clues. In time Tim Jr. came across a box of sand with a lid on it; he lifted the lid and there, scrawled across the sand, were the words "Regard dans les canons." He dropped the lid, yelled for me to follow him, and went tearing off into the night.

But before I could get out the door, Jody stopped me and told me it was a prank. As it turned out, Dave and Jet had set it up and he'd already fallen for it. So, what's a dad to do? I stood in the doorway laughing my head off as my son raced around the grounds checking all the cannons. But he took the prank in stride and we ended up having a great evening together. It was a good close to the day. Finally we all bedded down, anticipating the next leg of the race.

Staying the night in the fort was a reminder of how life so often has unexpected twists in store. The leaders in the race had thought they had a huge lead on those of us in the back of the pack; we were seriously concerned about not being able to catch up; and there was that equalizer awaiting us all. As I work my way through life's battle with Parkinson's, I take a lesson from these events. Don't ever give up. During the race we never knew for sure what would happen until we were standing on the mat, trying to prepare emotionally for what Jon was about to tell us. Were we the last team in? Was this an elimination round? Was he about to send us home? We never really knew, even when it seemed certain. So don't ever give up in life until, well, you're dead. You just never know when that next equalizer will show up and change everything.

Of course, those are easy words to say and much more difficult to live out. However, they remain true. We were so lucky so many times in this game, but we continued to get lucky only because we kept getting up each day and doing our very best. That best didn't always look pretty, but we continued to try. We chose to stay in the race, both physically and metaphorically. We didn't give up and just allow ourselves to get booted out. We kept our heads as best we could.

This is my hope for you: that no matter what you're facing in life, you'll have the strength to do your best every day, no matter what that looks like. And as you do, remember to have fun. By this point in the race we'd settled down and begun to enjoy the ride, and it was paying off.

We got up the next morning after having slept on the fort's hard concrete floor. Our next clue, we were told, could be found somewhere on the grounds. With that send-off, a day of disaster began.

We couldn't find that clue to save our lives. Time and again we'd walk into a room, search it thoroughly, and not see a thing. Then another team would walk in behind us and come right back out with the clue. It was maddening. At one point Tim Jr. had looked all through a filled-in well in the courtyard only to have Brett come up behind him, jump into the well, and emerge with clue in hand. We were so frustrated.

Finally, we ran through an opening in an interior wall of the fort and found our clue. It was outside, on the other side of a locked gate. So back out we went, way around the wall, up a steep hill, and down the other side to the opposite side of the gate. Well behind now, we were instructed to head for the ferry to cross the St. Lawrence River and find the founder of Quebec, Samuel de Champlain, out in front of the Fairmont Château Le Frontenac.

We frantically hailed a cab and made it to the terminal where—wouldn't you know it?—Brett and Holly and Jody and Cory were waiting for the next ferry. The boats left thirty minutes apart, and there they sat. Once more, Lady Luck had shone upon us. Still, if we'd despaired and dragged our feet, it would have gone differently. So we settled back and waited for the ferry, knowing that at the very least we were in a three-way tie for last place.

Now, that doesn't sound very positive. But again I want to highlight the fact that we didn't really know where we stood. We didn't know the other teams had all made the crossing; we merely assumed they had. Our day had been such a struggle, we'd been so wrapped up in the moment, that we'd overlooked the possibility that we weren't alone, that we'd actually caught up. It's in these frustrating moments in my own life that I try to remind myself of this reality: I don't know the full story yet. I don't know what's waiting for me around the next corner. The race continually surprised us with good things, and I want to assume the same for my life with Parkinson's. So despite the struggles, the hardships, the endless days where it seems you're just barely hanging on, let's remind each other that we do have the ability to hang on. And if we choose that, we'll be surprised by the good things that will eventually come.

By not making assumptions about the future I can focus on doing my best today. I'm not comparing it to yesterday or any possible tomorrow. It's an attitude that can lead to a real sense of peace because it allows me to develop true gratitude for where I am in life right now. Today, I could be depressed about having come down with Parkinson's; I could be fearful and dismayed over what my future may hold. Or I can spend a bit of time writing, as I've done on this particular morning, and then go join my family relaxing outside. Two vastly different perspectives.

Your life may look very different from mine, but I'm guessing there's something or someone you can focus on that's of far greater value than dismay or depression. Clinical depression or serious illness can't be swept aside. But we can focus our will in a positive fashion and direct it at those things we can control.

How do we play the cards we're dealt? All we can do, really, is carefully, honestly survey our situation and make a deliberate decision to grow where we're planted. This isn't an easy task; it's far simpler to give up and float along with the tides of life. Parkinson's has no cure. Why should I even try? I'm not going to get better, in fact I'll get worse, so what's the use?

I answer these questions from a place of faith—from a belief in a creative genius who cares about my future and will look after me. That may not be true for everyone. But I answer these questions based on my lived experience as well. No one ever expected the Tims to survive this race, yet leg after leg we

continued on. Here we were, in leg six of that incredible journey, having struggled all the way but still in the race—and
having a great time.

This is how I choose to live my life. Whether life is a
struggle or not, I will persevere. I'll fight back against this
disease and believe that I can live and die well with it. And
should I be so fortunate as to see a cure in my lifetime, I'll be
one of the healthiest and happiest guys waiting in line. Luck
comes to those who stay in the race.

The nature of perseverance, luck, and good fortune in life
generally—this was much on my mind during that ferry ride
across the St. Lawrence. Sharing the ride with the Docs and
Jody and Cory had me feeling great that we weren't alone at
the back of the pack. We were off to find Monsieur Champlain
and, it turned out, to have a regrettable encounter with a
mailman.

Upon our arrival across the river, we could choose
between two challenges: ice carving or finding and replacing
the missing details on a large mural. Unlike the other two
teams, Tim Jr. and I opted for the former. The missing pieces
were in French, and although Tim Jr.'s French is quite good,
we'd had enough of complicated challenges. We were sticking to our game plan.

We made our way to a beautiful European-style courtyard
and set about sculpting a house out of a block of ice. The sun
was shining on the cobblestone streets as we donned our gloves
and took up our chisels in an attempt to create a masterpiece.

As our block of ice slowly melted, we worked to satisfy the judge so that we could move on. We were almost done when Holly and Brett, having completed the mural challenge, ran by. When they yelled out that something-something wasn't far away, we assumed they were talking about the next clue.

With the sculpture complete, we were directed to the Place de l'Université-du-Québec. Having no idea where that was, we popped into a nearby shop and were told that it was about twenty minutes away by cab. Not only did that contradict what we thought Brett and Holly had said but the shop owner seemed unsure of her directions. So Tim Jr. and I decided to get a second opinion, at which point we came across that mailman. Now, if you were lost in a new city, I think you'd agree that asking a mailman for directions would be a reasonable thing to do. He informed us that the site was about five minutes away by foot, which lined up with what Brett and Holly had said, so off we went.

It would have been a great plan had he been right. I have no idea where he was trying to send us, but it wasn't where we needed to go. And much later in the day we learned that Brett and Holly hadn't been referring to the next clue; they'd actually said "The boys aren't far away," meaning Jody and Cory were right behind them. We wasted a full hour looking for a destination we were nowhere near.

At last we found a tourist-information kiosk and were given the exact same directions the shop owner had provided. We grabbed a cab and were finally on our way. We knew we were in trouble.

Sure enough, when we arrived all the teams were well into the next (and in this case, non-opt-out) task: making crepes, two savory and two sweet. Tim Jr. elected to take this on, his experience (limited as it was) being a better bet than my complete lack thereof. He was doing a great job following a local chef's instructions, but this was another challenge that required supreme attention to detail.

Meanwhile, first Dave and Jet headed off and then the other teams slowly melted away, leaving us with Celina and Vanessa. Vanessa was busy at work, demonstrating in the process that cooking was perhaps not one of her premier talents. She spoke a bit of French but couldn't figure out the last ingredient, so as she headed back to her griddle one last time she asked Tim Jr., "What does 'cerises' mean?" Without a moment's hesitation he responded, "Cherries." And with that she finished the task and left us on our own.

You have to understand that this is the kind of guy Tim Jr. is: he's caring and kind; he'll help first and think about himself second. How can you be mad at a guy like that? So I wasn't upset, but I still wished he hadn't said anything.

The devil is in the details, as the old saying goes. Eventually, Tim Jr. figured out that he was leaving the icing sugar off his sweet crepes. With that correction made, the judge was satisfied and we were finally given our next clue.

At this point we'd been alone at the task for a while and were starting to feel the pressure of finishing in last place—again.

The next challenge involved making a couple of passes and scoring a goal on a lacrosse field. That was easy enough, but there was no one else there. The clue after that directed us to find Jon at the mat—and now we knew for sure we'd be last. Any joy we'd been feeling earlier in the day rapidly dissipated.

Later, when the show aired, we'd hold a weekly viewing party with friends and family, often using the event as a fundraiser for our local Parkinson's chapter. For this episode we were watching from the neighborhood's Boston Pizza. The lounge was jammed and we'd overflowed into the restaurant. Everyone was having a great time—right up until the point where we got lost following the mailman's directions. When that happened, the restaurant got pretty quiet.

Then, as we finally came running up to the mat, the room burst into what I now refer to as "the loser clap": the rhythmic, polite version that audiences reserve for those whom they respect but nonetheless regard as losers. I realized then that no one was surprised. It was as if the entire room had expected our elimination. And who could blame them? Never had we given them any reason to believe we'd be successful. Leg after leg we struggled—and not only with my Parkinson's but also with our inability to even read a map.

But if you watched the show you may have noticed the goofy little grin we were wearing as we came to the mat that day. You see, we'd done the math and were convinced that this would be another non-elimination round. (I know, we could have been so wrong.) So during the loser clap that evening in Boston Pizza, we stood there like gods—we knew the future.

When Jon informed us that once again we were the last team to arrive, the disappointment in the room was palpable. But then he said those magic words: "I'm sorry to tell you, but your wives are going to have to wait a little longer to see you—this is a non-elimination round and you are still in this race." The room exploded in cheers and applause: everyone was thrilled and amazed that the Tims had somehow dodged the bullet yet again. I ran around the restaurant high-fiving everyone as if we'd actually won the whole thing right there and then. For me it was one of the greatest highlights of the entire experience.

The sheer joy of surviving when everyone is convinced you're done is a high that's hard to recreate. To experience that kind of thrilling success with friends and family is beyond words. And not only was the moment incredibly fun but I learned a very important lesson from it.

After all, in everyday life, how often do we hear the loser clap playing in our heads and simply choose to give up? We've all experienced some version of that repeating soundtrack: *you're not fast enough, you're not pretty enough, you're not smart enough, you're not strong enough.* Now, it could be argued that the Tims were any number of these things during the race. And yet by choosing to persevere, we went further and did more than anyone had expected.

If at any point we'd taken a step back and given up, no one would have judged us. No one would have questioned why our spirits flagged, why we were sent home. Had we just floated along and chosen not to do our best, no one would have noticed a difference. Rarely did our best look that great, so few would have questioned our demise.

But back in leg three we'd made that decision to follow the advice of my kindergarten teacher and just do our best. In the face of ridiculous odds, we chose to keep moving forward. It sounds trite, but that attitude took us much further than anyone would have imagined.

So when the loser clap starts playing in your head, stop and remember that. We chose to continue even when there was little hope for success. There was a championship with our name on it; we had only to stay in the race and go get it.

You can do more than you think if you're just willing to try. Whether I'm speaking in a classroom or a boardroom, this is the message I share: our best is good enough if we have the courage to see it through. Don't ever give up on yourself. I guarantee you'll be amazed at how far your best will take you.

So here we were at the end of leg six and, against all odds, still in the race. There was a lot of racing yet to be done, and our last-place finish meant we were going to face another Speed Bump.

Our next destination was Iqaluit, Nunavut, a cold and, to us, menacing land: my Parkinson's was about to be severely tested.

chapter 13

I'm Going to Need a Hand

I SUPPOSE I SHOULD HAVE been more worried than I was.

We headed into leg seven with a certain calmness, despite our back-of-the-pack position and the gut-level dread that added venom to the challenge of getting an extra task done. Nonetheless, we were off to Iqaluit to experience the far north—and to drop in on our competitors, who no doubt thought we'd been sent home at last.

Not many people travel to Nunavut, so there are very few flights. For the Tims this was great news because it meant that all five remaining teams would be on the same plane going north. At the airport we were met with grim faces— I believe it was at this point that the other teams started referring to us as "cockroaches," in the sense that nothing seemed capable of killing us.

Upon arriving in the frozen, hauntingly beautiful landscape of Iqaluit, our first task was to get an Inuktitut clue translated into English. It directed us to the Sylvia Grinnell

Territorial Park, so we grabbed a cab and headed out in search of it. Suddenly our cabbie pulled over and jumped out of the vehicle.

"Where are you *going*?!"

He muttered something about a washroom. All I could think was, *Are you serious?*

To his amazement we bolted from the cab and grabbed another. After all, we were the ones who needed to go.

Once we got to the park we were instructed to don parkas, wind pants, and boots and then set off across the tundra to find two Inuit women throat singing. After we stopped to take in the eerie sounds, the women gave us our next clue.

We made our way down a long hill, where I put on a pair of snowshoes while Tim Jr. jumped into the bright-yellow sled waiting there. Once I was ready to go, I grabbed the rope and pulled him a hundred meters across the snow to where we were to throw harpoons at bull's-eyes. With great effort I got the job done.

Now it was Tim Jr.'s turn to pull me back across the snow—a leisurely ride that I quite enjoyed. Along the way I noted how he seemed to manage the trek much more easily than I had. It wasn't until I watched the episode, several weeks after the race, that I noticed Tim Jr.'s position in the sled as I pulled. He'd been sitting at the front, cheering me on, all the while inadvertently burying the nose in the snow. And here I thought it was just youthful strength that made it so easy for him.

Back at the starting point, we took off on a snowmobile for the short ride to our dreaded Speed Bump—a task that turned out to be super fun. We were the only team that had the awesome opportunity to jump on a dogsled and mush a pack of huskies across the ice. Aside from one dog who had the most frequent urges to empty his bladder of any dog I've ever seen, it was a great experience.

Now we were on our way again . . . with the Girls. Just as we'd ended our dogsled ride and hopped back on our snowmobile, they pulled up on their machine. So we set out together across the ice to search for the oldest Hudson Bay building still standing in Canada.

Arriving at the old settlement, we were given the chance to allay our hunger with ten pieces of muktuk, which is whale blubber with the skin still attached. Tim Jr. and I had that agreement where I'd take on the eating challenges, so I sidled up to the table and dug in.

The first piece made me gag. I tried to swallow it whole but the skin, which is tough and chewy like black licorice, had very sharp edges to it. The fat was, well, fat. It slid down nice and easy. The next bite I took resulted in the skin and fat separating. Now I had the equivalent of two multivitamins in my mouth. But with the water provided, I managed to take my medicine.

What does muktuk taste like? I couldn't tell you. However, Celina choked, gagged, and wretched her way through all ten pieces, trying to chew them up. Ask her. I'm sure she has a good idea.

With snack time over we set out on the last section of the day. Our next clue instructed us to run a kilometer and find Jon at the mat. I was so excited! Running was something I could still do at this point in my life. Plus, I knew that only

Jody and Cory were ahead of us, and that we could outrun the Girls if we had to.

"Let's go!"

Roughly five hundred meters into our one-kilometer run, we made a bit of a right turn and saw Jon. He was standing at the top of what seemed like the tallest mountain I'd ever seen. My heart sank, the day's work settling on me like a heavy blanket of exhaustion. I wasn't sure how I was going to make it up that hill.

In that moment all things Parkinson's kicked in. I was already tired, and now I began to shake in earnest. Sweat poured off my forehead under a bright sun that brought the temperature to a brisk minus fifteen Celsius. My left foot suddenly couldn't get its toes off the ground, so I kept stumbling.

With our run having slowed to a crawl, I became obsessed with the fear that the Girls would overtake us. In my mind's eye I saw all the teams catching up, with Tim Jr. and I somehow ending up in last place once again—all because I just could not get to the top of the hill.

I eventually stripped off the Canada Goose parka we'd been given. Its rating was to minus thirty Celsius, which was excessively warm just then.

It became an overwhelming struggle just to put one foot in front of the other. Finally I broke down and said the words no father wants to say to his son.

"I need a hand."

Tim Jr. didn't draw attention to it and never missed a beat. He simply told me to grab his jacket and hold on. In this fashion we kept moving. Flags had been placed along the route, and at every second one we'd stop so that I could catch my breath and anxiously ask if anyone else was coming. At each stop Tim Jr. would wait patiently for me to settle while answering my ceaseless queries.

On this day my twenty-three-year-old son pulled my forty-eight-year-old butt up a mountainside. He brought us in at second place when many had expected we'd be in last. Instead this was the day we lost our good friends, the Doctors. This nonphysical team had faced two very physical tasks that got the better of them and led to their elimination.

Looking back on this leg of the race, there are a couple of ways that scenario could have played out. I didn't have to ask for help. Many others in my place might not have, but my desire to win overpowered any misplaced sense of pride. I don't think there are many fathers who'd relish the prospect of asking their kid to help them out, and I'm sure some kids would find it difficult having to help their father in the way Tim Jr. did that day.

But neither of us wanted to lose.

I saw in us an ability that I wouldn't have had on my own. I saw the opportunity to go further and faster together than I could solo. Once I set my pride aside, I realized that we're family, after all, and it's our job to help each other.

It reminds me of when Tim Jr. was just two years old or so. Sheryl and I were struggling financially at the time. My job wasn't going well and I had yet to gain any postsecondary education. So we decided that I'd drop what I was doing, that we'd both look for new jobs, and that I'd get into school.

I went back to waiting tables and, trust me, that was a move up financially. Sheryl got a job at an optometrist's office. This arrangement had me working mostly evenings and weekends and Sheryl during weekdays. The result was that I looked after Tim Jr. for the majority of his waking hours.

I'll never forget when he started crying for me as I'd leave for work. And if he was hurt or sad, it was me he'd run to. In my mind little kids would always run to their mom at those times; rarely would they cry for Dad. So this made an indelible mark on me, and changed the way I interacted with my son. I came to understand that he needed me in ways I hadn't understood before.

In Iqaluit I had the opportunity to experience this in reverse—and to learn how I sometimes need my son in ways I hadn't anticipated.

I hated the idea of losing more than I did the idea of asking Tim Jr. for a hand. We were a team, and we'd made the decision that each day we'd do our best. My best on that day meant first going slow as I pulled him across the ice and then relying on him to help me up the hill.

Our best isn't always what we dream it will be. But on that day my best involved embracing the team we'd become and giving my all to the task at hand. Could I have made it up the hill without Tim Jr.'s help? Sure, eventually. Would we have come in second place? Probably not. Third? Fourth? I don't know. What I do know is that I performed better, we placed better, and I became a better man that day because I trusted my team, my son.

These were powerful lessons, and I take them forward now in my struggle against Parkinson's. Just as on the show, in life I need a team to help me run this race.

There are days when it feels as if the team is making me work a bit harder than I'd like, but then I hear their voices cheering me on. There are times when I can't find the strength to put one foot in front of the other, and someone comes to lend a hand. Whether it be my wife, one of the kids, my support group, my physicians (GP, neurologist, psychologist . . . I have a few), or even a member of an audience to whom I've spoken a word of encouragement, there are so many who help give me the strength to run this leg of my race, to stand up to this thing called Parkinson's.

I am so extremely proud of what my son and I accomplished that day in Iqaluit. I'm also proud of the opportunity I've now been given to stand with members of the Parkinson's community and shine a light of hope into the darkness of this disease.

It's in community that we thrive. It's when we lay down our pride and place our trust in others that we find hope and comfort. We need our people, our community.

As I persevere, I'm gaining the ability, even learning the joy, of resting in the warmth of community and being at peace with my situation.

chapter 14

Is
That a
Big Deal
Here?

WITH EACH NEW MILE EAST across Canada, Tim Jr. and I reached a new personal travel record. Our arrival in Halifax for leg eight marked our first time in the Maritimes, and being the Midwestern landlubbers we are, the two of us should have known there'd be challenges ahead.

Along with the other remaining teams, we headed out to the airport parking lot to find our vehicles—in this case a shiny new manual-transmission car for each of us. Of the four teams, only Celina and Vanessa didn't know how to drive a stick. I'm glad I'm not the one paying to replace the transmission. From city street to highway they never got out of second gear, and once we got to Pier 21, they complained that the car smelled horrible!

It's said that about one in five Canadians can trace their family's arrival to Halifax's Pier 21. This Atlantic seaport has often been compared to its American cousin, Ellis Island. Hundreds of thousands of immigrants have found their way into Canada through its doors. But it was closed when we arrived late that evening, and wouldn't open until six the next morning. We were allowed in, though, and found sleeping bags set up around the room. After coming to terms with the fact that all our panicked efforts to get there had been for naught, we began to settle in for the night.

Just to have some quiet, Tim Jr. and I set up camp a little way away from everyone else. As I sat back I watched Jody Mitic slip off his prosthetics and then peel back the compression stockings he wore over his stumps. To those observant enough to notice, there were sores on those stumps—we nurses call them "pressure ulcers," but they're generally known as "bed sores." They develop in the elderly from lying in one position too long, although in Jody's case they're caused by the pressure and movement of the prosthetics. Pressure sores hurt, a lot. I've never had one, but over the course of my career I cared for many who suffered from them. Jody, however, never flinched. He took out the bandages he'd come prepared with, cleaned and redressed his wounds, and the next day got up and raced as if those sores didn't exist. To this day I remain amazed by this man.

As I fell asleep on the floor of Pier 21 that night, I saw the images of thousands of migrants making their way across vast oceans. I saw men and women from all walks of life sleeping on the floors of ships, hoping to remain safe. They carried with them dreams of a better future, of hope and security in a land far from home. I imagined the fear of parents for their children and the thrill that only a child can know of a great adventure in the vast unknown. I fell asleep with a heart full of gratitude for the many sacrifices these people made to make this country the wonderful place that it is, and for the men and women who now serve, protect, and defend the great country that those immigrant families built.

Our move to Canada was in the fall of 1989. I'll never forget the day I was standing at the kitchen sink doing dishes and looking out the window. I saw something peculiar and asked Sheryl if there could be a fire nearby, since there appeared to be ash in the air. She came over to the window, chuckled, and then informed me that what I was looking at was snow. The date was September 21. I had no idea it snowed in summer in Winnipeg. Then, having discovered that I was going to be cold for the rest of my life, I ran into culture shock. These Canadians looked like Americans, and although they were enamored with hockey, their football was basically American (minus one down). But to my dismay they didn't think like their cousins to the south; they even enjoyed bashing Americans. People often seemed to be telling me how the U.S. was wrong about some point. I can look back on it now and smile, but at the time I was truly lost. Like Dorothy and Toto, I was definitely not in Kansas anymore. As silly as it sounds, it led to one of my first bouts of, if not clinical depression, then something awfully close.

In many ways I think our migration to Canada, even though it was only from the U.S., likely mirrors that of some immigrant families. It was terribly hard, as I talked about earlier. We struggled, we almost failed, and yet we ultimately prospered in our new home.

Those first years in Winnipeg began the lesson in perseverance that I'd later need in facing Parkinson's. We're not one of the more glamorous cities in Canada, and we have our struggles. It takes a certain grit and determination to thrive here, but thrive you can. This city has a heart of gold that embraces people from all over the world. Its winters may be cold, but it has a very warm heart. Just to bug my friends who move away I've always said, "Only the strong live in Winnipeg; the rest move to British Columbia."

Our forebears walked into difficulty because they needed to, had to, desired to create a better life for themselves. They chose the dangerous path of crossing vast oceans and uncharted continents. I can take a lesson from that: if I faithfully walk my own uncharted, difficult path, I too may be rewarded with great success. We'll never know unless we set out on the journey and persevere to its end.

I had the chance to walk through the Pier 21 museum—to study the photographs and look into the eyes of those who'd made the perilous voyage to Canada. I couldn't help thinking of the perseverance that must have taken. I can't imagine the poverty and deprivation some would have experienced, the hardships many would have suffered. It must have been a long, lonely journey as they traveled to reconnect with loved ones— and some would have lost loved ones along the way. Others may not have wanted to make the trek in the first place, having been forced out of their homes and countries. It's hard to appreciate the full extent of these individual circumstances and what it took for them to keep moving forward.

For many, what at times must have been a very dim hope was all they had: the hope that at the end of that long journey life would get better. It's often difficult for the individual living with Parkinson's to look to the future with hope. Yet imagine with me those immigrants making their way from Europe to

Canada on a ramshackle vessel. Suppose they were to greet each morning with a "What's the point—I'm just going to die when I get there"? We wouldn't think much of their ability to endure, to hold to the hope of a brighter future. While in no way dismissing the struggles of today, I believe we must hold to the hope of a bright tomorrow. We don't know what the future holds. Why would we waste today by worrying that tomorrow may not be all that we hope for? It may just surprise us and be far greater.

We woke up to a stunning sunrise. From Pier 21 we needed to make our way to Mahone Bay—except that we had, of course, lost our map. So while Tim Jr. frantically searched our belongings, we just followed Jody and Cory. They were pretty ticked off about it; we chased them for quite some time, and all the while they did their best to lose us. After finally finding the map, we left the guys—and then beat them to the next task. We took great pride in that.

The folks of Mahone Bay put on a fantastic, if slightly creepy, scarecrow festival each year, and our task was to create a twin of one of the scarecrows. Once Tim Jr. had completed it, our next challenge was a choice between catching lobsters and something to do with sausages. I've mentioned before that I'm not a big fan of the water, let alone fishing—only in recent years have I come to appreciate seafood—so we opted for the latter. On arrival we found that we needed to memorize the names of twelve different types of sausages. Tim Jr. was not excited by the prospect. We each took half, concentrating on the peculiarities of each type of sausage and their unique German names. Then, reasonably satisfied with our efforts, we raced off to find the butcher.

That butcher was clearly shocked when we rattled off names like "Schweinefleisch" and finished the assignment in one go. How in the world did two guys from Winnipeg pull this off? It helps that one has been long married to a German with loose Mennonite roots. And you wouldn't guess it by looking at me, but it also helps that I'm half German, which apparently comes with an inherent ability to distinguish sausages. I suppose adaptation also plays a role. Growing up in Kansas, I didn't know about things like perogies or farmer's sausage; not a single one of my siblings would have eaten something called "borscht." But like many other immigrants to Canada, I've come to appreciate not only the rich mosaic of cultures that make up the country but also the foods that go along with them. Especially those of the German/Mennonite variety!

Our last decision that day was whether we should U-Turn another team again. In the end we opted not to: the U-Turn board listed us in second place, and we weren't really feeling any threat from the teams behind us. Now we needed to figure out the relevance of our next clue: a Canadian dime. There was some kind of ship on it, but I'm a Midwestern boy—what I know about ships could be written on one side of a, well, dime. It turned out that the ship was the *Bluenose*, a celebrated fishing and racing schooner built in the 1920s in Nova Scotia. It had become a provincial icon. Tim Jr. asked on camera, for all of Canada to hear, "Is that a big deal here?" Yes, it's a big deal here. Our task was to find its successor, the *Bluenose II*, which we did with the guidance of some local folk.

The next stop on the race was Port aux Basques, Newfoundland and Labrador. I was glad Sheryl trusted me, because I was about to engage in some serious flirting and some heavy kissing. I was also about to learn what it means to be "screeched in."

chapter 15

Screeched

In

LEG NINE STARTED with a foot race to three vehicles. The first two would carry one team each; the third would carry two. They'd each leave fifteen minutes apart, giving the lead vehicle a thirty-minute head start over the last. Tim Jr. and I wanted vehicle number one. It was ours. We knew we could beat the others in a foot race—a guy running on prosthetics, two bulky weight lifters, and two young ladies, no problem. We'd spent the last number of hours strategizing: this was our chance to come out ahead; this moment had clearly been scripted for us. Parkinson's or not, I could outrun every other person left on the race except for maybe Tim Jr. We were pumped and ready to take a commanding lead.

We'd traveled overnight by ferry to get to Port aux Basques. That morning, four teams came barreling off the boat to reach the terminal entrance doors all at the same time. Pushing and shoving, we fought to get through. These massive men struggling to pull open doors that opened outward were crushing the Girls. I was genuinely concerned for their well-being and pushed back against the other guys.

Once we were all inside, we found that the terminal was under construction. On the right was a plywood wall with a single door, and so another struggle to get through ensued. The young bucks had pushed the old man, me, to the back, which gave me a wider view of the room. A quick glance to the left revealed another set of doors! Now I'd seen the vehicles— they were directly out those doors and to the right. I did the math: through the doors, a hard right, then across the parking lot. It was slightly longer, but I was much faster. I can do it! My body tilted into full swing for the doors, but as my gaze swept right to left I noticed the look of concern on the terminal guard's face. And was she saying "No!"?

I bolted for the door, through two sets of glass, a hard right, and into a full sprint. There were the vehicles . . . behind a seven-foot-high, barbed-wire-topped fence. I ran back through the terminal and jogged quickly toward the cars. There was no rush—I was last. Rather than the commanding lead we'd envisioned, we were, once again, firmly at the back of the pack. I had to explain it all to Tim Jr., who was at first perplexed and then upset (something of an understatement there). I couldn't blame him. This was entirely my fault.

In silence we made our way to the Terry Fox memorial that commemorates the starting point of Terry's journey across Canada. We read his famous line, "I just wish people would realize that anything's possible if you try; dreams are made if people try." We were trying, Terry! It was this quote that we had to memorize to get into our first-ever Newfoundland house party.

I'd never been to a party quite like this one. When we and the Girls got there we were instructed to kneel. This alone was disconcerting. Then a reasonably fresh cod was produced, and we were told that we had to kiss it. Only later did I learn that this lovely fish had seen a lot of lips that day. Every other team had had their lips on this cod's kisser; that is, except for Jet, who was given the privilege of kissing its other end (they decided to have some fun with him). Our lips were then cleansed and our bellies settled with a shot of rum. This rite of passage apparently completed our welcome as true sons and daughters of Newfoundland. We had been officially "screeched in."

I'm not sure whether it was the rum or the fish, but as we made our way to our next challenge, Tim Jr. began to warm up to me. We chose the task that involved walking a massive Newfoundland dog. Now, this dog was the size of a small pony and drooled like my old grade nine buddies had over their Farrah Fawcett posters. Our job was to load up a wagon with eggs and milk that the dog would tow around. Without breaking the eggs or spilling the milk, we had to deliver them to a number of different homes.

I started off leading the dog. Before we go any further, I need to tell you that I don't like big dogs, or at least most big dogs. As a kid delivering newspapers, I had a gigantic collie take a bite out of my favorite jeans—an event that has forever turned me off big dogs. And drool? Nurse or not, I don't like human drool, let alone dog drool. I think our Newfie could sense my lack of enthusiasm. She refused to move.

Enter the dog whisperer. Tim Jr. has a kindness of spirit and a gentleness about him that have always amazed me. He's one of those guys who can walk into a place and immediately have a room full of new friends. He takes a genuine interest in people, and has an easy grace around those who might otherwise be left aside. Once I'd relinquished the leash to Tim Jr., our Newfie seemed to instantly sense all this: her tail began to wag and away we went. I trailed behind, trying to preserve the milk.

The next thing I knew, the dog whisperer had propelled us from last place to first. We'd caught up to Jody and Cory, and when they had to replace some broken eggs, we passed them. They didn't seem too happy that we'd come storming in from the back of the pack like that.

So we ended up being the first team to leave that stage of the race and the first to arrive at O'Brien's music store. I was vaguely aware that we may be in the lead at this point, but I was more concerned about my task: I needed to choose something from the store with which I could raise fifty dollars by busking on a street corner. The prospect made me nervous: I'm not really musically inclined, I don't play any instruments, and I certainly don't sing. Panic was starting to well up in my gut when I spotted some juggling equipment. Juggling balls! Way back in the day when I worked at youth camp, my buddy Dave had taught me how to juggle three balls. I grabbed a set and headed off into the streets of St. John's.

There I promptly set about doing one of the things I do best in life, which is talking. While keeping my three balls aloft I regaled citizens with tales of a "brown man from Winnipeg juggling on the streets of St. John's." Of how it was a sight to behold and was surely deserving of their support. I begged, I bellowed, I pleaded, and I flirted with every middle-aged woman I could find who would listen to me. In the end it was four charming ladies who donated the last few dollars I needed to put me over the top. So with all my charm and wit, you'd think we'd have been first in and first out of this task, right? Not so.

Jody had arrived at O'Brien's after we did, and then proceeded to the street to tell war stories of bravery, great loss, and survival. How do you compete with that? Then Celina showed up wearing a bright pink T-shirt and carrying a hula hoop with a bright red ribbon on a stick. (How this all fit in a "music" store I never figured out.) Now I was downright worried, and with good reason. As soon as she began to swing that hula hoop, the contest was over. Finally Dave arrived; by then I was truly scared. Dave, a natural entertainer and funny man; Jody, a war hero; and Celina, well, I don't have any of her talents.

I was thinking that I'd soon land in last place all over again. So I talked faster, juggled harder, and flirted my way to that fifty bucks. But by the time I had my cash Celina was gone with Jody right behind her. Then, on my way back to the music store, I noticed an interesting thing: Dave, the natural entertainer and funny man, wasn't being all that funny; he was having a rough time. So while Dave struggled on, I put my head down and ran for the store.

Our final clue instructed us to find Jon at the most easterly point in North America. We grabbed a cab and took off. We were in the semifinals now, and in third position. All we had to do was make it to the mat and we'd be racing for half a million dollars in cash and prizes.

And then we got lost.

Our cabbie said he knew right where to go, so when we arrived we jumped out and ran toward what we thought was the light—in this case, the literal light of the lighthouse. You see, we hadn't asked the cabbie which way to go, nor had we stopped to read the signs posted right next to the road that indicated where exactly the most easterly point was. We just saw the lighthouse at the top of the hill and ran for it. It turned out that Jon was nowhere near the light, so we ended up running all over that hill looking for him, all the while in full panic that Dave and Jet would arrive and take our third-place spot.

Finally, we stopped and looked down over the edge of the cliff: Jon was far below. Tim Jr. took off like a shot, yelling for me to follow. But I was tired by then, and still nervous about Dave and Jet catching us—which, together, made me shake, which in turn made me afraid that I'd fall on the steps leading down. (It didn't seem reasonable to have these concerns at age forty-eight, but there it is.) To make matters worse, the stairs were of that widely spaced, awkward variety where you need to take a step and a half to cover each one. It was hard to run and time them correctly; Tim Jr. and I actually had to stop and have a brief argument over his having to slow down. And, of course, he did. He understood.

In the end, we beat Dave and Jet to the mat. It was a sweet win, but with a bitter edge. We found it really tough to see them eliminated—they were great guys, and it had been a blast watching them have so much fun on the race. But then the reality set in: we had survived the entire race and made the top three. We were going to be racing for the championship! How in the world had that happened?

The truth is, we'd gotten to this point in the race because of Tim Jr.'s ability to set aside the frustration he'd had with me that morning. It was a big deal that I'd altered the plan and messed things up at the airport. Having struggled throughout the entire race, we'd genuinely felt that it was our time to take the lead, and that didn't happen. A lesser individual could have harbored that bitterness and let it affect the rest of the day, but not Tim Jr. He was able to accept me and the (wrong) decision for what it was and move on. And not just move on but excel. Really, his dog-whispering charm was on display all day. Empathy and understanding were his responses to my inability to keep up. He respected me as an individual, faults and all, and stayed focused on the task at hand.

There's a lesson to be taken here, I believe. Parkinson's has thrown a number of wrenches into my life. It makes a constant and concerted effort to mess things up. Like most people, I had a plan about how my life would go. That plan never involved a chronic, debilitating disease. I never planned on having to worry about falling down a flight of stairs at forty-eight. Can I, like my son, set aside the frustrations of things not going the way I wanted them to and stay focused on the race? Can I move forward finding charm, even peace and joy, when things aren't going well? Can I find grace and understanding for myself when my body just won't work right? Parkinson's is a horrible, insidious disease, yet I can take a lesson from Tim Jr. in how to live my best with it. My life is not about Parkinson's, no matter how much it might seem to be. There's a bigger, brighter life to be lived. At times, I just need to be reminded of that.

Having been raised in the American Midwest, my child-hood was inundated with stories and movies about cowboys. Although I loved the old westerns of John Wayne and the like, the lonesome, solitary figure they often portrayed never resonated with me. And as I've grown older, that old "pull yourself up by your bootstraps" mentality has made less and less sense. In fact, I don't think I can point to any truly self-made man or woman. Oh, I know, it's a glamorous idea, and we may want to believe it, but no one truly experiences success of any kind solely on their own. From the Warren Buffetts to the Mother Teresas of this world, they always have a team alongside them. That team may be in the shadows most of the time, but they exist nonetheless.

Any success I've had in life has come with others' help. Whether it's Sheryl or Tim Jr., I've come to learn that I go further that way. I've also learned that I don't like to admit this. I often seem to feel that I've somehow failed if I ask for help or even acknowledge that I need it. Then I remind myself of that old saying, "Iron sharpens iron": the notion that we grow and mature when we're in relationships with people who can not only challenge us but also encourage us to be more than we'd be on our own.

It's that empathetic friend who may never have gone through what we're going through and yet who remains at our side, encouraging us to keep moving, helping us see the brighter side of life, even physically lending a hand as needed. The amazing part is that each person is helped in some way—that whereas help seems to be flowing in only one direction, it's in fact flowing in both.

Sheryl and I have found this when we've done service

work in third world countries. We anticipate being a help to the people living there, but come away having been encouraged in what feels like far greater ways.

None of this is to say that we don't have a responsibility for our own well-being, but rather that we'll experience far more success within a caring, giving community of like-minded individuals. That act of slowing down long enough to take in the plight of others makes our personal world a better place.

It never looked as though Tim Jr. and I would succeed, yet here we were, heading into leg ten—the final leg of the race.

chapter 16

The Win

WE'D MADE THE TOP THREE, but with an emphasis on the number three. Tim Jr. and I started the day with the sense of being well behind Jody and Cory, who'd now won three legs in a row; they were on fire and looking to take the championship. Regardless, we were thrilled to have made it to the last leg. There was absolutely nothing that could diminish our spirits. We were amped up and ready to go.

That morning I reflected on how far we'd come from the outset, when I'd been so desperately concerned about embarrassing my kids. We'd survived two non-elimination rounds along with the extra tasks they required. We'd faced my Parkinson's on a daily basis and persevered through its challenges. We'd failed miserably at so many junctions and yet here we were, standing proudly at the beginning of the final leg. Words cannot describe the joy, relief, excitement, and myriad other emotions I was feeling.

Whether or not we'd win this thing hadn't entered my mind that final morning. Okay, that's crap—my mind was reeling with the thought that we now had a one-in-three chance! But equally strong was the simple thrill that we'd done what no one had thought possible. We'd made the top three alongside two petite young women, who hadn't seemed like much of a threat at the start, and two brothers, one of whom ran the race on prosthetics. You can't make this stuff up.

From Cape Spear, Newfoundland and Labrador, we made our way to Canada's world-renowned city of Toronto. It was here that the final chapter would be written and the victors crowned. After Air Canada bumped us to first class (thanks, guys!), we arrived in TO and got ourselves to the L Tower, a brand-new, fifty-seven-story building that was still under construction.

Jody, Vanessa, and Tim Jr. were taken to the top and harnessed in: they'd be rappelling fifty-seven stories straight down, face down. Trust me when I say how jealous I was—I'm not afraid of heights and would have loved to rappel like that. But Tim Jr. also really wanted to take this one on, so I gave him the opportunity. This turned out to be one of the better decisions we made on the race.

It was fun watching from the ground far below as Jody, the burly military sniper, made his way down the side of the building. Was that a touch of concern I saw in his eyes? Vanessa, meanwhile, was full-on terrified. Then there was Tim Jr., grabbing at the guide wire and yelling to be allowed to go down faster. Attaboy!

Once he was on the ground we were given our next clue, which led us to the factory where the Cadbury chocolate bar is made. Walking through those doors and taking in the fragrances was pure heaven. But then came the task.

After we'd put on white coats, hairnets, and gloves we were instructed to take one box of chocolates at a time, open it, and look for a solid "gold" chocolate bar. That sounded easy enough. I'm not sure this fully played out on television, but the task turned out to be maddening. My tremor wasn't all that bad at the time, but it was just bad enough to prevent me from easily opening the individual wrappers, especially with the gloves on. Finally, after much frustration, I figured out the trick.

It took a lot of chocolate boxes, but at long last Tim Jr. and I were the first team to locate the golden bar and receive our next clue. Which is to say, we were in first place for the first time on the last leg of the race.

Giddy with that thought, we headed out to the Toronto Zoo. On the way we chatted with our cab driver, who mentioned that a big panda exhibit had just come to town. We'd been instructed that our next clue wouldn't be found in any of the "animal enclosures"—but since this was an "exhibit," it seemed like a reasonable place to start. Off we went to check out the new arrivals.

We did have a look around, but in the end we didn't go all the way in; by this time we'd concluded that an exhibit was the same as an enclosure. We spent the next hour and a half blowing our lead. Only after speed-walking through every single square foot of the zoo did we determine that maybe, just maybe, we should have gone into the panda exhibit after all. An enclosure is where the animals *live*. An exhibit is something else.

Somewhere on the trek back to the pandas we met a young lad who, with the type of sarcasm only a twelve-year-old can muster, freely informed us that "It's in the pandas, guys!" Evidently he figured he had a good idea of what we were doing and what we'd missed. "Yeah, great, kid," I thought. "Where were you an hour and a half ago?" Still, somewhat encouraged, we continued on to the exhibit.

Once there, we made our way through to the other side—where, lo and behold, sat the clue box. It became immediately clear that the other teams had come and gone. Our one luxurious first-place moment had gone up in a cloud of smoke. Yet again we were in that familiar back-of-the-pack position.

Throughout our lengthy journey around the zoo we'd had to continually talk each other down. We were desperately worried about the other teams passing us (as, it turned out, they did). But we kept reminding each other that we knew something the others didn't: the flags and flowers we'd been noticing throughout the race. With no real justification, I held on to that belief. We just needed to get out of there. So, as difficult as it was not to lose our minds in the zoo, we held tightly to the hope that we had an ace up our sleeve.

The next clue instructed us to head to the Evergreen Brick Works (where I'd be stepping up; whoever hadn't done the rappelling challenge had to do this one). So we hopped in a cab and made our way across town to this farmers' market, café, and all-around beautiful outdoor space in the middle of the city. As we pulled up, we were still hopeful that, just maybe, one or both of the other two teams had struggled in the zoo as well.

Nope. As we hauled our bags out of the cab I spotted both

Vanessa and Jody sitting outside. To say they were thrilled to see us would be an understatement—they'd been convinced we had come and were long gone. The height of their joy was matched by the depth of our despair. They must have been there for at least an hour already.

Still: those flags and flowers. I think I'm generally a good judge of people, and I had a strong, gut-level hunch that neither of these teams would have noted those clues as we did.

You'll recall that, before we even left for the race, my wife had instructed us to pay attention. Again and again she stressed the need to note the small things on the journey—and that the end of the race would likely feature a task requiring our having seen or memorized something along the way.

That's why, when I noticed British Columbia's provincial flag on the very first clue, a little voice went off in my head: "Pay attention!" I heard that voice again on the mat at Quails' Gate Winery, where the greeter standing beside Jon was wearing a small white flower on her lapel. From then on, a flag and a flower appeared every day of the race. And every evening, Tim Jr. and I would sit down and commit them to memory.

So when I walked into the Evergreen Brick Works that day I felt extremely hopeful. Inside, Celina and Cory were already working at the task. There were three giant maps of Canada—so big that we needed a ladder to reach the top, and each arranged to obscure the view of the other competitors. We were given two stacks of placards, and—you guessed it—one featured flags and the other flowers. We were to place each image on the corresponding province or territory we'd visited throughout the race. It was like hearing angels sing!

I started off with what I was certain I knew: the flags. Then, feeling confident that I'd placed them all correctly, I moved on to the flowers. These were trickier. I'd spent a lot of time memorizing their names, but not so much on their characteristics—and the placards showed only the images. So I took my time. It wasn't long before I realized that a number of flags bear the provincial or territorial flower.

Steadily working through them, I came down to the Northwest Territories and British Columbia, each of which is represented by a white flower with multiple petals. Which belonged to which? I could only take a stab at it. Then I hung all the placards and asked for the judge—who took a long look and then informed me that my map was incorrect. Still feeling sure about the flags, and mostly sure about everything else, I switched those last two flowers and called for the judge again.

And that was that. Not just done, but done in two tries and about twenty minutes.

Tim Jr., Vanessa, and Jody were just settling in for what they assumed would be a long wait when I came bursting out of the building. No one could believe I was already done. Tim Jr. was baffled; Vanessa and Jody were, of course, concerned. We were back in first place, and with the end of the race so close, maybe for good this time.

We were down to the final clue: find Jon at the mat on Centre Island. There's nothing like rush-hour traffic when you're in a hurry. Tim Jr. and I had hailed a cab and were now crawling our way across town. I was sure I was going to have a stroke as we traveled at a snail's pace to the ferry.

Once we were within a couple blocks of the terminal, our

cab driver told us to get out and run for it. The ferries departed every half hour, and he thought that if we hustled we might just make the next crossing. So we jumped out and sprinted off, all the while scared to death that the Girls would somehow, once again, catch up to us.

We went screaming into the terminal, making all kinds of demands for information and tickets. I have to say, the ticket guy was pretty rude—he told us to settle down and that we still had eight minutes until the next ferry. Did he not know the gravity of the situation? Those were the longest eight minutes of my life.

To pass the time and try to figure out where we might need to go once on the island, we studied a map on the wall. Given our generally poor record with maps, we used the full eight minutes to try to understand the island's layout.

At last the iron gates opened and the crowd began to file aboard. You would have thought this was some kind of tourist event with people milling around taking pictures. I just wanted the captain to hit the throttle and get us out of there, but no, we had to wait for the kid with the ice cream cone.

Finally everyone was on board. Tim Jr. was excited but I felt more cautious; the gate remained open and the Girls could still make it onto the boat. Then the gates closed, the ferry's drawbridge went up, and Tim Jr. was seriously ready to celebrate. No, I said: the Girls could still stop the boat or make the jump from shore. At last the engines throttled up and we pulled away from the dock. When we were a good twenty feet out and I felt convinced that the Girls couldn't make the jump (seriously, I was that worried), I told Tim Jr. to let the celebrations begin.

But my moment was quite different from his. For the first time in weeks my world went quiet. Even my body and the constant shaking went still. I kept thinking, "We could win this thing." No one else had made the boat. We were in first place with a huge lead. The boys who were constantly lost just had to find Jon.

We had thirty minutes.

As the ferry came into dock we made sure to be the first to the ramp. Tim Jr. and I pressed hard against the gates; no one was getting off that ferry before we did. Fortunately, the crowd seemed to realize something was up and gave way.

The ramp came down, and at last the gate swung wide open. We bolted from the ferry like inmates suddenly freed from prison. Sprinting into the park, we quickly came upon the little bridge crossing a stream. Then, once across the bridge, we were into a large expanse of green leading us directly to the water's edge.

And the mat.

The clap line had already formed, with those racers who'd already been eliminated arrayed in two lines on either side of the mat, cheering us on. The Twins, who'd gone out in the first leg, seemed to be the loudest, crying out "Way to go, boys!" The Cowboys greeted us by swinging their signature, if invisible, lassos over their heads. Together, our fellow racers created a passage for us straight to Jon and victory.

We dropped our backpacks and flew across the field. There were high fives all around. Jon greeted us on the mat, this time alone, and with a huge smile on his face. I couldn't wait to hear the words I knew would come. What Jon said next led to a joy and celebration matched by only a very few moments in my life.

"Boys, you are team number one!"

Finding the right words to describe our feelings in that moment is extremely difficult. We'd come from behind so many times after having barely held on. I've said it before: we never doubted we could win, but we never really thought we would.

Aside from the birth of Tim Jr.'s daughter, this was the most incredible moment I've ever shared with him. He was and is a wonderful teammate, and I'm so thrilled that we had the chance to make these memories together.

After a bit of time we were joined on the mat by Jody and Cory and Celina and Vanessa. All nine teams went on to celebrate this amazing journey we'd had the pleasure of experiencing together.

Finally I got the chance to call Sheryl and tell her the news. Of all places, she was standing in line at Walmart. She later described the scene: how she was screaming and crying and yet unable to explain herself. This was, of course, still our secret; the entire race had to be run on television first. She left the store quite sure that everyone around her thought she was nuts.

Of course, she's anything but nuts. It was her insistence that got us to apply for the race in the first place. It was her "I guarantee you'll get an interview" and the remarkable insight that "they'll love your Parkinson's" that started us on this journey.

I'll be forever grateful for Sheryl's admonishment to *pay attention*. It was this advice that ultimately made all the difference. For all the husbands out there, let me just say that if there's ever a time I was glad to have listened to my wife, that was it! In the end, we didn't entirely live up to the twins' "Don't embarrass us" request, but I hope the win made up for it.

chapter 17

Jody
Mitic

STANDING ON THE FINAL MAT, our race done, we waited for the last two teams. After having spent so much of the race at the back of the pack, it was a unique situation to find ourselves in.

It became clear that we'd managed to get a fair lead on the others. But in time Cory came blazing over the bridge, followed closely by Vanessa. Two beats behind her was Jody, and then Celina. Jody had switched out his shoes for prosthetic running blades and now came flying across the park toward the mat, giving me one last chance to stand in awe of how he handled his disability.

Jody's run was in some ways reminiscent of Terry Fox's run across Canada, but in other ways it was completely different. Terry hadn't had the benefit of today's technology. The carbon-fiber blades Jody wore, combined with his warrior spirit, made him a formidable sprinter, one whom Celina couldn't catch. That day, Jody and Cory came in second.

A grueling, twenty-three-thousand-kilometer race across Canada won by a guy with Parkinson's, with second place going to a guy running on bilateral prosthetics: if the bookies had only known! I don't think anyone would have predicted that ending.

Which takes me back to the first day I saw Jody. It's a humbling admission, but I'll never forget how quickly I dismissed his ability to compete. We were in a hotel banquet room, each team at their own table; we weren't allowed to talk to one another. But we were, of course, checking each other out.

That's when I caught sight of the prosthetic on Jody's right leg. I mentioned it to Tim Jr., noting how it could be a hindrance. A while later I noticed the prosthetic on his other leg. My reaction was purely competitive. Do you remember being told not to judge a book by its cover? Well, in that moment I hadn't recalled Mom's sage advice, which proved to be a dumb move on my part.

I did, however, determine then and there that, whoever this guy was, if he could show up and compete on bilateral prosthetics, I could compete with Parkinson's. He lit a fire in me; I thought, "If he can, I can." Jody proceeded to kick my butt pretty much every step of the race.

There was a time when I would have likely described him as "disabled," but that's not at all accurate. I'd now watched him complete tasks with prosthetics that many "able-bodied" people could not.

Jody Mitic is a living example of strength, courage, and perseverance. We weren't racing alongside each other at the beginning, so I didn't see him walk the plank off the train bridge in Kelowna. When I watched it later on TV, I was dumbfounded. How did he not fall off? My first thought was that he looked like how I'd felt; that is, shaking to pieces. So I couldn't believe how calm I appeared and how wobbly Jody was. At that point I realized that he was walking the plank several hundred feet in the air on what basically amounted to stilts—and then he had to kneel down to retrieve the clue.

Remember that other task in Kelowna, the one that involved riding out on Jet Skis in search of Ogopogo? Jody couldn't wear his prosthetics—he might have lost one or both in Lake Okanagan—and since he couldn't mount the Jet Ski without his legs, Cory piggybacked him there. With Jody sitting at the back, they took off across the water. I'm not sure just anyone would allow themselves to be carried to a Jet Ski, set down on it, and then driven out into a lake, not to mention doing it on national television.

Later I witnessed the skin sores that had developed under his prosthetics as the race wore on. At Pier 21 I'd watched him tend his wounds and then slide his legs back on. Locked and loaded. His determination was inspiring.

Throughout the course of the race I felt that Jody and I had the same attitude toward giving up: we wouldn't. Over time I witnessed a number of emotions in him, ranging from anger (when we followed them until we figured ourselves out) to that gentle look and tone that only a father can produce when talking about his little girls. No matter what he was doing, I had the sense of a continual commitment to never stop, never bow, never give in to the disability that clung to him.

Jody lost his legs while serving in Afghanistan. I'd like to share with you that story, which he tells in his book *Unflinching: The Making of a Canadian Sniper.*

Jody and his fellow soldiers had gone out on patrol one night to observe a village near their base. The team had made their way around a cemetery filled with Taliban fighters and had cut across a farmer's field. They came to an opening in a wall that looked to be the best way through—although, Jody recounts, the most obvious path in a battlefield is often the most dangerous.

It was a dark night. Equipped with night-vision goggles, they had spread themselves out to avoid putting the entire group in harm's way should something go wrong. The lead soldier went through the opening, ensured that the area was clear, and motioned for the others to follow. Each soldier in turn cleared the entry and took up a defensive position. Jody was the last to go through. But as he cleared the entryway . . .

"I turned and took my first step forward. My right foot touched the ground, and a massive orange fireball soared across my face. I didn't hear a sound. For a few seconds, I felt weightless, as if I was suspended in space.

"The next thing I knew, I was on the ground. My ears, nose and mouth tasted like mud. And that's when the pain hit, a pain so intense it completely overwhelmed my body and my silence. I started punching the ground and screaming, 'Oh my god! Oh my god!' It was the only time in my life that I'd ever uttered anything religious."

There had been two land mines packed one on top of the other. The rest of the team had managed to miss them as they crossed through the same space. That night Jody lost both legs, and nearly his life, simply because he stepped on the wrong spot. He goes on to recount his survival, his recovery, and what motivates him to never give up. It's a marvelous story.

And it's a testament to the fact that we all have our stuff to deal with. This is Jody's, mine is Parkinson's—yours could be anything. It's not the things in our lives that ultimately make the difference, but rather our attitude toward those things and how we choose to respond to them. Jody can't go back and not step on that land mine. My Parkinson's isn't going away. Your thing may never get better; in fact it may get worse. So then how, and why, do we find the strength to move forward?

Throughout the course of the race I never heard Jody complain or "play the disability card." I honestly don't think he even considers himself disabled. He has a plan, a purpose, and a will to live to the fullest, all the while walking through life on carbon-fiber feet.

When I face difficult days with my stuff, I often think of my beginnings—since if we're to see our way forward more clearly, we need to spend time understanding our past. I'm reminded of that little half-breed boy and how so few held out any hope for him. I'm reminded that there were parents who took me in and made me their own. Back then, and since that time, God has given me far more than most would have ever imagined. That in turn gives me great confidence that my future will be just fine as well. Even with Parkinson's.

I sense that Jody and I come from very different walks of life, that we may see the world through different lenses. Yet I have the utmost respect and regard for this man, who has served his nation and nearly paid the ultimate price for it. It was my honor to have raced alongside him, and I continue to be inspired by his ongoing battle. So when I have bad days with my Parkinson's, I often think of Jody, of his strength and courage throughout the race.

He will forever remain among those who inspire me.

chapter 18

Coming
Home

THE CELEBRATION STARTED on the mat that afternoon in Toronto and spilled over into an after-party with all the racers and the entire production crew. By one in the morning I was utterly exhausted. Despite the excitement, I had to call it a day.

And what a day it had been! I couldn't imagine that life could possibly get any better. And with the race now done, my heart and mind turned toward home.

It had been about a month since I'd seen Sheryl and the kids, and I couldn't wait to share our stories in person. Tim Jr., too, was anxious to get home to his wife, Kara. So despite our exhaustion, it was exciting to be heading back to Winnipeg. But as we sat on the plane an unsettling thought began to form in my mind: I now had this really cool secret that I couldn't share with anyone. Only Kara and Sheryl knew, and that would remain the case for some time. It was going to be a long six weeks until the first episode aired on TV, and longer still until the final episode.

Sheryl and I had already decided not to divulge the final results to our other three children. The frustration this created in our house was incredible. But no season of *The Amazing Race* had ever been spoiled by someone revealing its outcome. And since the show's producers had instructed us to be hypervigilant about social media, we thought it best to remove any possibility of a slipup. Still, we hadn't anticipated what a burden it would be to keep the secret.

When it came time to return to work, that burden turned into a real nuisance. I couldn't talk to anyone! My colleagues knew I'd gone on holiday, and so asked the usual "How was your vacation?" questions; I made up what I thought were lame-sounding lies. When I said that I'd done some traveling with my son, most just looked at me oddly. I guess no one travels with their kids these days, or perhaps I'm just a lousy liar. I often got a puzzled "Really, where did you go?" I'd say something like "Oh, you know, around the East Coast. We've never been there," and so on. Most people seemed a little confused, but thankfully they let it go.

We tried hard to settle back into life and carry on as if everything was normal. But nothing was normal. My boss at the time was one of the few who knew where I'd gone. From time to time she'd give me a "So, you going to tell me or what?" look. Who could blame her?

It was even worse at home. The kids were relentless. Always asking, always trying to trick an answer out of us, to find the subtle meanings behind things said. It was mentally exhausting. Never had I been in a situation where I couldn't freely share my joy. Parents know that you don't tell your kids everything in life, but this wasn't the kind of secret we wanted to keep. Still, it all had to wait.

At long last the date for the first episode was announced; finally the season-one teams were about to be revealed. True to race form, we were announced dead last. The irony was not lost on me.

With the revelation that a team from Winnipeg would be among the contestants, the love and support we received throughout the next months (and indeed years) began to flow. The excitement ramped up slowly but grew perceptibly, day after day and week after week.

If I had a dollar for every time I was asked whether we'd won, I could have retired multiple times over. The daily questioning of some colleagues bordered on harassment. I was forced to continually duck and evade. And the longer we stayed in the race, the more intense the scrutiny became.

As the first episode approached we began to get asked whether friends and family could watch it together. My first thought was how fun it would be to hang out with a group of people, experience the race together, and be able to witness everyone's reaction to our win. Then I recalled our poor performances *before* the win: we'd have to survive nine episodes of them. I wasn't sure I could stand it—two non-elimination rounds, getting lost in practically every leg, often coming in last, shaking like a leaf in the wind with my Parkinson's. In the end I said no to a party, at least for episode one. First I wanted to see how we'd be portrayed: Would we come off as the show's idiots who just happened to pull off a win?

So we wrapped ourselves in the comfort of family to see what would become of us on national television. Now, we're part of a rather large family. A good number of us gathered in the basement of my sister-in-law's place and huddled around the television. It was a benign enough event. No one openly mocked us for missing the second clue in the butter-flies and the subsequent thirty-minute penalty. We ended the first episode in sixth place out of nine. Overall, not stel-lar, but not horrible either. Nor were we characterized as the show's idiots, which was reassuring. I had to admit that our characterization was pretty fair: they told the truth, warts and all, just as it had played out.

As we talked afterward, it came to light that they had a family pool going; bets were being placed. Only one niece had backed the Tims. Heartwarming bunch, this family of mine.

We decided to try a friends-and-family get-together for the second episode a week later. We met at a local pizza place and all but filled the lounge. Week after week these little gatherings grew, forcing us to find venues that could hold the crowd. We had a great time with old friends and the many new friends we made along the way.

For me, the two most memorable events were our non-elimination rounds. For the first, we rented a local theater so that we could watch the show on the big screen; a local pop-rock radio station hosted. The place was packed. By this time Tim Jr. had moved to Fredericton, New Brunswick, so he sent a video saying hello to the crowd and thanking them for their support. We charged for the event, with the funds going to support Parkinson's. The second non-elim was that epi-sode where everyone was giving us the "loser clap" at Boston Pizza, so experiencing its ultimate success with friends and community was particularly fun.

There was one event I couldn't attend, which I still regret. It was, of course, the last episode. We needed to be in Toronto to watch it with a live studio audience, and although our immediate family was there, we missed the group of friends and family we'd become accustomed to. Meanwhile, we'd had so many requests to hold a viewing party that before leaving for Toronto we made arrangements for one at our church, this time with a local classic-rock station doing the hosting. Apparently, the place was crazy all evening. When we got lost in the zoo everyone was on the edge of their seats, thinking we'd blown it. Then, when we came running across the bridge, the place went absolutely nuts. I so wish I could have been there to celebrate with our community.

Sometime early in the show's airing we began to get other requests. One of the first was from Matt Sutton, a personality on the local radio station 99.1 Fresh FM. Matt was a fan of the show, so we came up with the idea of doing a weekly spot, called "Tim's Take," where I'd share my thoughts on the previous week's episode and bring about more awareness of Parkinson's disease. Matt and I even carried this format into season two of the race, even though I wasn't part of it. I greatly appreciate the support that he and the station gave me and the Parkinson's community.

As the show reached its end, the phone rang more and more with opportunities to tell my story and advocate on behalf of people living with Parkinson's. One of these came from Parkinson Canada, asking that I give a short presentation at the World Parkinson Congress in Montreal. Over three thousand people from around the world would be attending, including researchers, people living with Parkinson's, their care partners, and the Parkinson's community at large. I was thrilled to share my five-minute speech with this incredible audience.

And I had no idea that that five minutes would launch a speaking career that would take me around the world. I've since had the privilege of speaking to companies, schools, churches, and of course myriad Parkinson's-related entities. So in many ways the race hasn't ended for me, but rather taken on a new life. It has broadened and deepened my community.

Whether it's a school assembly or a hospital association, many are curious about what Tim Jr. and I did with the prize winnings. Without fail, three questions almost always lead off any question-and-answer session. Especially among young men, the first question is, "Did you keep the cars?" A new 2014 Chevy Corvette would have looked great in my driveway, but neither Tim Jr. nor I kept the vehicles we won. The main reason is that Winnipeg is known not only for its lengthy winters but also its horribly potholed city streets. Besides, I still had three kids at home and needed a new minivan. And since our contract hadn't stipulated that we accept them, we took the cash value instead. With deep gratitude to Chevrolet Canada, a cool fifty-five thousand bought a "new to me" minivan and a trip to the French Riviera.

The next most popular questions are about either the $250,000 or the ten trips for two anywhere in the world Air Canada flies. We didn't do anything exciting with the cash; it went toward clearing any debts we had and paying down the mortgage on the house. As for the trips, Sheryl and I took the other three kids to France for three weeks as a primer.

Then the two of us went to Vietnam and Croatia. (Tim Jr., meanwhile, went to Chile, Japan, and Australia.) It was an insane amount of travel to squeeze into thirteen months—and was made possible only through the good graces of my employer at the time, St. Boniface General Hospital. They were extremely kind in granting me leaves of absence to allow us these fantastic opportunities. I'll be forever grateful for that.

One of the most meaningful aspects of the race has been sharing it with others. I've had great opportunities to speak to so many different audiences, from a group of business leaders to a group of individuals with Parkinson's to a single family. Together we've celebrated not just the race but the ability to overcome what appeared to be insurmountable odds. I've been told by countless individuals that our achievement has inspired them in facing and overcoming difficulty in their personal lives. So many parents have told me how the show (and our performance in particular) became their weekly family time—a commitment to hang out with their kids and, ultimately, celebrate together.

I've never experienced community quite like I have in Winnipeg over these past few years. It was, of course, a neat experience being on television and radio shows, being the grand marshal in the Santa Claus Parade at Christmas, and receiving the key to the city from the mayor. But more than anything, it's been the people themselves. Sometimes I'd be stopped in the hall at work—going to work was basically a waste of time for the first few weeks after the race, and was never so much fun. I was even stopped in the mall a bunch of times and asked for a selfie. Everywhere I went people wanted to celebrate this really cool moment in time.

St. Boniface Hospital pulled out all the stops and threw a huge party in the middle of the workday, allowing me to cele-brate with all my colleagues. I was so stunned and grateful for this awesome gesture. Words cannot describe the amazement I felt to have friends (and my bosses!) standing in line to receive my autograph and take a photo. It was an incredibly fun day.

And then there was the most surprising celebration of all. I'd always ridden my bike or bused to work. On my first day back I'd gotten up feeling a little out of sorts: the event was over, and here I was, going back to my job. But I'm a lousy morning person anyway, so I stumbled through my usual rou-tine and made my way to the stop for my 7:16 bus. When it arrived I stepped on and paid my fare. Then, just as I turned to walk to a seat, the bus erupted in applause! For a moment I didn't know what to do; I was embarrassed and thrilled at the same time. Fortunately, I gathered my wits enough to share my thanks with the group. As I sat down, there were two of us on the bus who felt perplexed: me—the guy who couldn't believe how lucky he was to be living in this kind of town—and the poor guy I saw lean over to his buddy and say, "What did I miss?" These are my people, my community. This is my city. I don't know where life will take me, but no matter where I go, Winnipeg will always be home.

chapter 19

Live
Your
Best

HOW DO I GO ABOUT SUMMING UP the Live Your Best concept? I never want the conversation to sound trite, or dismissive of the very real struggles we face; I never want to sound as though I'm saying that if we just try a little harder it will be all right. The fact is that sometimes things are not all right. Sometimes things go horribly wrong and we're left broken, wounded, suffering in the face of great loss. We're in a fog of doubt, wondering how we can go on.

Bad things happen to us all. In everyone's life, the sun shines and storms rage. Sometimes we can understand the storms and their purpose, but at other times we're left aching for answers to the question "Why?" The important thing, though, is how we choose to respond to the hardships that enter our world.

So my hope in all this is to offer guidance that we might hold on to in the face of the storm. Like any skill, perseverance can be learned and honed. When we practice these seven lessons, we're never far from safe harbor.

LET GO OF THE HAPPINESS MYTH

What's the difference between happiness and joy? Happiness is an ice cream on a warm summer day. Joy is infinitely more than being made to feel good by our circumstances. I like this definition by Rick Warren—that joy is "the settled assurance . . . the quiet confidence that ultimately everything is going to be alright." An ice cream on a warm summer day can never bring about that kind of feeling. Living through hardship and coming out the other side can.

Suffering, if we allow it to, can draw us deeply into an ability to persevere. Hardship can teach us how to stay in the race even when all seems lost. It can teach us how to hold on when we feel as if we can go no further. I'll never forget standing on the mat at the end of leg three, having come in last place. Even when we didn't end up being sent home, part of me just wanted to quit. Sometimes we wish the struggle we're facing would just go away. Mine was the threat of humiliation and my ongoing battle with Parkinson's. What is your struggle that you wish would go away? I would encourage you to name it, and to walk hand in hand with it. Discover the means to stay on your journey and win.

I said earlier that we've been sold a lie: the lie that we should pursue only those things that make us happy. As my daughters have grown up, I've often told them not to believe the lie of all those beauty ads that promote a fake, unnatural look and an unrealistic size for most women. I say the same here in our context: don't believe the lie that our lives should be free of pain and hardship. Life just doesn't happen that way. Think of the many grueling, difficult tasks that we have to work hard through and that ultimately lead to joy. Those triathletes who daily slog through the intense training of three demanding sports with the hopes of one day becoming an Ironman are a great example of embracing hardship. Are those athletes always happy to swim at five in the morning in a cold pool? To run fifteen miles in the rain? These things don't always bring them happiness, but they often produce joy—the sense of having accomplished something meaningful, having overcome something difficult, having done what you didn't want to get up and do but did anyway. There is no joy without suffering. Do not believe the lie.

UNDERSTAND THE NATURE OF LUCK

You just might get lucky—and that's not being trite. During our race, Lady Luck showed up a number of times on our behalf. As I've said before, it's those who stay in the race who so often seem to get lucky. I can guarantee you this: give up and you'll never see luck. The truth is that none of us know the end of our stories. There are those times when we're convinced that there can be no positive outcome and we just want to quit. If that's not the time to persevere, I don't know when is. When you've gone as far as you can go, you gut it out and hold on. You persevere until you're thrown off the race, but you never leave of your own accord.

I was "lucky" enough to be in the ten percent of individuals with Parkinson's who are diagnosed before the age of fifty.

I was also "lucky" enough to be chosen out of ten thousand applicants to be among the nine teams to run *The Amazing Race Canada*. And how in the world were we "lucky" enough to win the race? I certainly don't believe that life is merely a bunch of random lucky moments. But whether you call it luck or divine intervention, there are many times in life when we're left baffled, scratching our heads, wondering how in the world something came about. Everyone experiences that. Then there are times when something extraordinary happens, and we're so grateful that we hadn't given up. Those moments come only to those who choose to stay in their race and persevere.

During the final task, it was such sweet success to stand in front of that giant map and know I had the information I needed. Watching it later on television was actually even better. As the race unfolded on TV, some on social media continually derided us as being merely lucky. It was often said that we didn't deserve to still be in the race, either because we'd hit the non-elimination legs or, for some, because we'd used the U-Turn. The flags-and-flowers challenge was our vindication.

Sure, we were lucky, but not with the flags and flowers. You either knew them or you didn't, and we knew them. Sheryl had reminded us to pay attention, and we had.

And therein lies an incredible life lesson. It reminds me of that old saying, "The harder I work, the luckier I get." We were lucky in the race, and it sure helps when we get lucky in life. However, we also worked hard. We'd made the decision to do our best. In the end, that was good enough.

Not only is doing your best all you need to do; it's all you *can* do. Sure, there are times when we need to stretch ourselves, to press more fully into a given task, but really, we're only ever trying to do our best. The race taught me to ask the honest question—What will my best really look like today?—and then work toward living that reality.

It's always the right decision to push hard, to work hard, to prepare and then lean into the task at hand. This is what it means to do your best. Included in that thought is the idea of simplicity. I tend to overcomplicate my life, to *strive* in making things happen. I've come away from the race with a greater appreciation of what it means to simplify my existence by understanding that this doesn't mean working less hard or relinquishing great aspirations. Rather, it means stripping away the excess in order to focus on what's most important. In part, this is what it took for us to ultimately win the race.

This is the foremost lesson I carry through life, now that I live with Parkinson's. With all I've been given in life, I feel the obligation to find ways to encourage others, and to live with as gracious an attitude as possible. When we get up and do our best, luck often follows.

ACCEPT LIMITS

Contentment. The word alone can produce a ripple of frustration in my soul: I imagine a quiet peacefulness that's at odds with what I often feel my life to be. I've known people who seem to inhabit that kind of space, and I've always wondered what it might be like.

I remember being sixteen and sitting on our front step one hot summer day in Kansas, bored out of my mind, wishing I was older and could take on all the amazing things that only adults get to do. I wonder if this doesn't represent the first seeds of my discontent. A restlessness that only now, many years later, is being tamed by Parkinson's, of all things. It's an unrelenting master. You may dance with it, but it will choose the music and the timing. At best, you can only follow along.

I've come to terms with this fact. That is, the nurse in me understands the clinical reality; I can say the words out loud without flinching. I've also taken it that difficult step further: I acknowledge that modern medicine cures very little and that I'll likely go to my grave with this new best friend whom I hate.

Surprisingly, this has brought me a level of peace, of contentment.

Sounds insane, I know. Does my acceptance of Parkinson's equal a lack of courage to move forward? Not at all. Instead it gives me a foundation from which to attack the future. I can't change the fact that I have Parkinson's. It doesn't mean that I can't live well with the disease and that I can't work for a cure. But until I accept reality, I'll never be able to successfully move forward and I'll never know true contentment.

What is contentment? Is it merely "a state of happiness and satisfaction," as it's defined? I think it's more than that. I think it involves a choice—but do you always have one? Yes and no. I can't choose to not have Parkinson's, but I can choose how I respond to it. The disease is a hard thing to bear, but is it any more difficult to choose contentment? Parkinson's has taken my ability to run as well as I did, but what good would it do me to daily lament that I can no longer manage a seven-minute mile? It seems like a silly notion. The disease has also taken my ability to function as a nurse—and of what value would it be for me to lament this loss? Yes, there is an appropriate mourning to be had, but at some point I need to move on.

Here's the hard part, the part that many people facing life-changing circumstances struggle with: "What can I do to remain productive and useful?" One practice I have is to list the things I can still do and then ask how these might be used to help others. I would encourage you to start your own list, keeping in mind that no ability is too small or insignificant to make the cut. Now, how might you deploy these to put a smile on someone's face or ease their burden?

When we take the time to draw up an inventory of our lives, we find that things may not be as bleak, we may not be as barren in ability, as we thought. We can choose to accept our shortcomings and embrace what we *can* do.

Our lives are finite. We all know we've been given a certain number of days; it's just that we rarely like to think about it. Parkinson's has driven this reality home. It has encouraged me to make good use of my time, knowing that it could be taken from me. It's a matter of being courageous enough to acknowledge that truth—and to recognize that our time is also infinite in the sense that every day we can choose innumerable ways in which we might live our best. The options before us are limited only by our imagination and our willingness to dream new dreams.

Early this spring, an arborist came by and inspected the magnificent old elm tree that had stood in our yard for as long as we've lived here. It was a truly beautiful tree, the largest for blocks, its branches extending into our neighbor's yard and creating a canopy over the street.

We were told that the tree had a major split down the center of its huge, bifurcated trunk and would need to be cut down. It was hard to believe: the tree looked healthy and strong, with no visible sign of disease. Nonetheless, it stood on city property and had to go.

We were dreading that day. Now Sheryl was in tears as we witnessed the speed and cold efficiency with which our tree was brought down. Giant branches came thudding to the ground; they were thrown into the chipper and all but vaporized. In short order our mighty elm was reduced to sawdust and chips, our yard left with nothing but little mounds of dust dotting the newly fallen snow. When our daughters arrived home from school they cried.

We'll mourn the loss of this beautiful tree, but in time we'll move on. It's inevitable. And it's necessary, even healthy that we do so. But that doesn't mean we'll forget; rather, we'll plant a new tree where the old one has fallen. This is what it is to Live Your Best—this is contentment in the living. We can't change the fact that the tree had become unsafe. So in its place we'll plant anew, begin a new season of growth. And that tree will bloom with a beauty that couldn't have existed had the old one not come down.

Parkinson's has brought a certain closure to my past life— you could say that it has felled it. But I can plant anew; I too can experience new growth and new beauty. By accepting limits and by practicing contentment, I can look forward to all that will be as I learn to grow in this new life I've been given. It won't look the way I had imagined, but I'm confident that it will be all that it should be.

As a nurse I've watched as individuals and families fight

hard against illness and even death. I've seen the frustration, the anger, the hardness that comes over people when they realize that they won't have their way over their ailment. I've watched them leave this life with sour, bitter souls, angry at the hand they'd been dealt. But I've also witnessed what happens with those who are content with the life they've been given: rather than feeling resentful about what they didn't have, they leave this world full of gratitude for all they did. The difference is striking, and it's compelled me to continually weigh my own life. And when its totality is placed in the balance, there's no reasonable response other than contentment.

That doesn't come easily to someone who's often been described as a Type A personality. I like to know where I'm going, to control the pace and the course. I've always had the sense that there are more challenges to be taken on and tasks to be accomplished. So learning to simplify my life is a daily struggle that involves all aspects of my being.

It helps to learn the boundaries of control—that I can still do many things, but in a more thoughtful manner. For example, because I think better early in the day, mornings are best for higher-level cognitive work. But that's also when I have more physical energy. And since I can't go to the gym every morning and get other things done as well, I need to stagger my morning activities over the week. So I do have some measure of control; it just looks different than it used to. And a big part of accepting limits is setting reasonable goals for myself each day. The choice is never easy, but it is simple.

CEASE STRIVING

Perseverance can sound easy—just don't quit. Well, not so much. There are times when we do need to quit things, thoughts, or even people who are no longer working for us. We need to push out or just let go of what's burdening our lives. These aren't rash, random actions, but rather careful considerations. What can I still do, what do I truly need to do, what must remain in my life, what can be let go? All with the goal of weeding out the unnecessary and bringing a sense of calm to our lives.

An important part of achieving such simplicity is the ability to cease striving. As Tim Jr. and I learned in leg three, striving is a destructive mindset. It can mean a panicked, irrational response to circumstances, a "damn the torpedoes, full speed ahead" approach with no thought of the consequences. That may make for great movies, but in real life it's seldom a good course.

To adopt a "cease striving" attitude doesn't mean that we no longer set goals or have a burning desire to succeed. It comes down to controlling those things that we can control. It's focused, deliberate action that takes into account the reality of our personal abilities. Parkinson's is profoundly adept at pointing out my limits, and I dare say that this can be a good thing: I can assess what I can and can't do and concentrate on the former. Have you ever wished someone would just tell you which way to turn or what decision to make? How many times have I wished I could still run home to Mom and Dad and have them guide me? Well, in a sense that's exactly what I have with Parkinson's. I may not always like what I hear, but the instructions are clear. Then I have the freedom to choose how I move forward. There is freedom of choice, there is control; it just doesn't always look the way I thought it would.

I've always been a little fascinated by those who seem fixated on youth, who strive not to age—those who maybe receive one facelift too many or one tummy tuck too far. Why don't they simply accept life for what it is? We all age; we just don't have to get old! But then I'm reminded of my early response to Parkinson's: I was adamant that it wouldn't put limits on my life. No disease was going to tell *me* what I could or couldn't do. I was in charge! Well, as they say, good luck with that. It's not an easy thing for me to do, but it's ultimately more satisfying to cease striving, accept my reality with Parkinson's, and live my best. And not only is it more satisfying but I end up accomplishing a lot, too.

TAKE EVERY ADVANTAGE

We do our best to set reasonable goals, but part of persevering is being ready when an unexpected opportunity turns up. Take the U-Turn. After we used it in the race, many howled that we'd been poor sports. Not true. It's a fair part of the game, and it helped us significantly. From time to time life will throw us a bone, a bit of good fortune, an out-of-the-blue chance—and we must be prepared to act on it. Now, life is not a game, and I'm not suggesting that we cause anyone harm, but rather that we take advantage of the good fortune that comes our way. It seems obvious, but we don't always do this. We feel we don't deserve or haven't earned something, or that it's unfair to receive when someone else hasn't. Here's my advice: take the gift and be grateful.

I'll never forget the humiliation I heaped upon myself one evening. Not long after Sheryl and I were married, we were helping to raise funds for the organization we worked for and had gone out for dinner with a couple we'd approached about a funding opportunity. The evening went well—until it came time to pay, and the couple offered to treat us. It should have been no big deal, but since we had invited them, I felt that we should pay. So I resisted the offer, to the point of offense. "What," said the man, "is my money not good enough for you?" That was a tad harsh, but the truth is I thought I had something to prove; I was insecure about not being in the same financial position as this couple; and a part of me felt I didn't deserve their generosity. Looking back, I physically cringe at how I must have come across. It was a simple gift, a bit of good fortune, and instead of graciously accepting it I made the moment horribly awkward.

Here's a story you may have heard but that nicely exemplifies the idea: A man trapped in his house by a flood begins to pray to God to save him. After he climbs to the roof, the floodwaters rising all around him, an individual in a boat comes by and offers to take him to higher ground. The man declines, saying that he's prayed and believes that God will save him. In time, he's swept away by the flood. Later, in heaven, he's upset with God and asks why he didn't save him. God's reply: "I tried."

Most believe they would never be as naive as the character in this story, and maybe they are right. Yet, time and again we were told that we should never have used that U-Turn. I, on the other hand, am so glad that we jumped in that boat and sailed to higher ground.

PAY ATTENTION

Sometimes recognizing those gifts isn't easy, which is why it's so important to *pay attention*. To this day I still smile when I think of the edge we gained over the other teams on the race; it was as if we had an unseen (and maybe slightly unfair) advantage of a third team member. Of course Sheryl wasn't there, but the advice she'd given was so profoundly important.

Pay attention: that can sometimes be an incredibly difficult task. After all, when we're under great stress, the mind doesn't function properly. So many times on the race when Tim Jr. and I were lost and confused, unsure of what to do next, we'd be told to "read your clue." I was continually amazed at how often we could do that and still not be any the wiser. When they told us to "read your clue," what they really meant was "*understand* your clue."

Understanding requires concentration and focus—which is so hard when you're under stress. Stress forces us to work too fast, which in turn makes us blow past the "clues" in life that we might have otherwise put to good use. So at these times I stop, collect my wits, and take stock of the situation. I look around my life and ask the important questions: Where am I at? Where am I going? Am I going where I want to go or should be going? These are just a few examples of how we can take a careful view of our lives and then become more deliberate about where our next steps take us. And when we learn to pay attention to the details in life, we often come away amazed at how things fall into place.

FIND COMMUNITY

As a husband and father, a healthcare professional, and a man living with Parkinson's, take it from me: we all need to ask for help sometimes. And that's a good thing. Many a Parkinson's fighter is drawn to isolation, just as many people suffering other hardships are. I find that, more and more, the most comfortable thing for me is to sit in a quiet space with no stressors that cause me to shake. It's always a temptation. If that sounds unhealthy it's because it is. We all need solitude sometimes, but I'm talking about a detrimental pull to aloneness, an isolation that prevents me from ever being challenged in my disease. I know I'm not the only one to feel this pull; I see it in others with Parkinson's all the time. We want to feel sheltered, safe, and free of any anxiety that will produce symptoms.

However, we need community. We need the friendship of individuals who get what we're going through. Who can not only sympathize with our difficulties but also call us out when we're slipping into unhealthy places. For me the important community spaces are my church, my Parkinson's support group, my exercise group, and U-Turn Parkinson's. Each provides the human contact that helps me see my life more clearly and respond better to both the world at large and my personal circumstances. In short, these are the places that give me the helping hand I sometimes need.

And of course, there's family. During the race, they were always with me—the words of wisdom from my wife, the support of my three younger children (excluding their concerns that I'd embarrass them), and Tim Jr. I could never have done those amazing, adventurous things without his help. Two moments in particular stand out for me. The first came when I admitted needing his help to get up that snow-covered hill. It was one of the more difficult things I've ever had to do, since I'd always thought parents were supposed to support their children, not the other way around. But in swallowing my pride and asking my son for a helping hand, we went further, faster. Anytime I'm afraid to ask for help now, I remember that. The second time was less obvious, but no less significant. It's funny to look back on it now, but at the time it was no joke when I took the wrong door out of the airport terminal and made us dead last. Tim Jr. was upset—and who could blame him—but he understood and he forgave, which helped us both move on. We all need to learn from our mistakes, but dwelling on them doesn't do any good. Slowing down to help others, and feeling empathy for them, can put you ahead in the end. Both parties, those giving and receiving help, get a leg up.

So yes, there are times when I need a hand. Sometimes I need friends to call on just to make it through the day. I'm so grateful for the gift of family, friendship, and a community that does just that: they help me get by.

These seven lessons, these attributes of perseverance, have led me to a place that deepens my character—that innermost person we find when we're all alone. I'm more grateful, more patient (this one's a work in progress), and more peaceful.

When I had to retire, I'd been a nurse for twenty-one years. It's always been in me to try to help people, from working with youth to my involvement with charities like Compassion

Canada. This aspect of my character development—the deliberate effort to get outside myself and be of some good in my world—is important to me. I need to be reminded (often at times, it seems) that I'm not the center of the universe and that I'm not the most hard-done-by individual on the planet, either. There are people who live under much worse circumstances. I need to find a way to give back that doesn't keep me in the spotlight.

In a fast-paced world, it takes a lot of effort to slow our personal lives enough to help ourselves, let alone those around us. Yet I've often been surprised by how much I benefit from taking the time to lend others a hand—it deepens, adds texture to, brightens, and matures me. It makes me more joyful and content with the person I am when I'm all alone. My character is changed for the better.

This is what it means to Live Your Best: To embrace the suffering that comes our way. To hold it close as our new best friend whom we hate. To keep going in the face of suffering and to allow the journey of perseverance to work into our character a new and better person.

Doing so leads to a startling conclusion: I find hope. Hope is realized in the fact that I can *live* with Parkinson's. In the fact that I can survive and even thrive in the face of it. Hope is realized in the fact that I'm made a better person in the course of the journey, that I *can* do this, and that I can leave my world a bit of a better place because of it. At the end of it all I discover hope. And that leaves me with a smile.

chapter 20

Speaking
Out

AS I WRITE THIS, the fourth season of *The Amazing Race Canada* is being filmed. It wasn't exactly announced, but when you have as curious a wife as I do, you learn these things.

It's hard to believe that three years ago I missed my twins' fifteenth birthday to begin this incredible journey. In the blink of an eye those three years have passed. The twins are graduating from high school, Tim Jr. and his wife have a beautiful baby girl, and the race continues to be a bright part of our lives in ways I never could have imagined.

Today, for example, I find myself in Scottsdale, Arizona, where I'm the keynote speaker at a retreat for individuals with Parkinson's and their care partners. The sheer variety of events I've been asked to speak at has been incredible. From schools, churches, and hospital associations to businesses and organizations around the world, this story has resonated with and touched so many lives. One of the most enjoyable of these events took place in Madrid, at a conference held by a pharmaceutical company. Sheryl and I spent five days taking in the sights, sounds, and sangria of that beautiful city. Talk about a poor kid from Kansas putting on the Ritz!

Of course, Parkinson's events have played a significant role in my newfound speaking career. An absolute highlight and honor was having the opportunity to present on the TEDx stage in Winnipeg. True to form—my form, that is—it also gave me another lesson in perseverance.

As luck would have it, one of the TEDxWinnipeg members, Marnie, rode my bus to work every morning, and one day, sometime after the race had aired, we happened to be sitting together. She recognized me, and after chatting a bit she asked whether I'd be interested in applying to speak at their conference. I was thrilled by the offer.

So I got right on it and sent in my application. This was going to be incredible! Not long after, though, I received one of those polite "Thank you for applying but, umm, no. Thanks anyway" replies. It was worded more professionally, of course, but that's how it felt. By that time I'd been doing a lot of speaking, with requests coming in from all over North America. Rarely was I the one doing the asking, and I do believe this was the first "no" I'd received. It did my ego some good, though: apparently I still stood somewhere off the direct center of the universe.

The next time we met on the bus, Marnie seemed a little embarrassed (and I was still a little flustered). But all was well, and we agreed that I'd try again the following year. As that year rolled around, the TEDxWinnipeg team did indeed ask me to speak. It seems they'd had the opportunity to get to know a bit more of my story and felt that it would make a good fit. I was over the moon once more.

I really wanted this speech to go well. I labored over the text; I struggled with the right wording and sentence structure; I wrestled with what stories to tell, how to use my voice, which positions to take on stage. I wanted it to be touching, moving, unforgettable. I'd wake up in the night stressed that the tone of the speech was off, that it wouldn't connect with the audience. I spent countless hours rehearsing and memorizing, determined that this would be a flawless presentation. In short, I was striving.

You'd think the biggest, most important lessons in life would stick the first time we learn them. But it seems that I, for one, need the same lesson a few times over before it really sinks in.

The day of the presentation was upon me and I was a nervous wreck. I'm not generally a nervous speaker. I love the stage, the crowd, the spoken word, the spotlight. But that day I was a mess. My TEDx coach and I had walked through the speech numerous times; I'd even practiced it on the stage. I should have been good to go, but in my mind I was still striving to make it happen. I couldn't relax.

As I walked out to rousing cheers, the heat of the lights hitting me, I was a ball of anxiety. I felt beside myself, as if I were somehow disconnected from my body. Nonetheless I launched into the speech. The crowd was engaged; they were laughing at all the right spots; it was okay. Then I completely forgot where I was going in the text. I had no idea what my next line was.

Fortunately, we'd planned for this. I'd stopped pacing at the bottom left of the stage, which happened to be directly in front of my coach. Standing stock-still and looking straight at her, I pleaded with my eyes that she throw me my next line. She understood. She called out the line and away I went.

It was all I could do to finish. I knew I'd blown it, that after all my hard work I'd made a fool of myself. The world now knew I was a fraud, a second-rate speaker who forgot his lines. As I exited the stage, it seemed to me that the applause was merely polite. I could barely get back to my dressing room and slam the door before I completely broke down. I think I freaked out my coach, who couldn't understand my distress. The rest of the day was spent in an emotional fog.

It took me months before I was able to watch the speech. (If you're curious, you can find it online.) Even then, the first few times I couldn't get past the point where I'd dropped the line. Many have since remarked that, had I not told them, they never would have known. They'd thought it was just a pause for effect.

On the day of the speech a number of people congratulated me, saying that I'd "hit it out of the park." I couldn't hear the words. Why? The burdens we place on ourselves. The striving to be something more than our best. Since that day I've often asked myself why I couldn't have just enjoyed the ride. Done my best and been content with what that produced. The only answer I've found is that I wanted that elusive *something more*. That hundred and ten percent that can never be had. I'd been unwilling to accept my best.

I've since come to feel proud of that TEDxWinnipeg speech. It's brought me many more opportunities to speak because, if you'll forgive me, it's really not bad. I've also come to use the speech as a reminder that my best is good enough.

That there was no need to put myself through the trauma I did that day. Time has proven that even on a bad day I can do pretty well. I'm so grateful to the members of TEDxWinnipeg, who gave me the opportunity not only to speak but once again to grow as a person.

I'm continually overwhelmed by the impact my story of the race has on others. From time to time I reflect that, had Tim Jr. and I given up at any point, the loss would likely have had an effect beyond just us. As it is, our perseverance has given me the pleasure of seeing others encouraged by our win. They've made it their own, drawing from it an inspiration that helps them face their particular "races" in an "If they can do it, I can too!" kind of spirit. It leaves me wondering what good things have come about in others' lives because we've chosen not to give up in ours. We think and act as though we live on separate islands, as though our actions impact no one but ourselves, but I've seen that this simply isn't true.

Perhaps the greatest impact has been an increased awareness of Parkinson's—and that effect is growing. I've been able to speak not only within the Parkinson's community but also to governments and the public at large about the unique needs of people living with Parkinson's. I've been able to convey that it's not just an old man's disease; it can strike individuals at any age.

And the more I'm able to speak out, the more I'm able to shine a light on the many services that are available to people living with the disease. A middle-aged man I met recently said that, for eighteen months after his diagnosis, he told virtually no one about it. He rarely even left the house. Then he found out about a support group—and was able to learn that he wasn't alone, that there are many like him struggling with the same issues.

As I look to the future, I keep before me the need to persevere—not a hard thing to remember, since every morning Parkinson's, my tenacious "friend," must be dealt with yet again. And as I look around at my family, I'm also reminded of the need to carry on. This remains our number one goal each and every day: regardless of the difficulty, regardless of how successful we feel, just keep moving.

We in the Parkinson's community don't know when, or from where, our next win is going to come. What symptom relief might be around the next bend, or when the cure may arrive. So in your job, in your family, or in that thing you just can't seem to get on top of, keep going. You can't know where the next breakthrough will occur.

We greet each morning with the intent to discover that day's win in whatever form it presents itself. On some days it's just the fact of having gotten up; on others it can be so much more. But the goal remains the same: seek out that next win and never give up.

Simply do your best. Your best will always be good enough; even in the face of difficulty it will be good enough; even when there's no evidence of success it will be good enough. There's a win waiting for you—you just have to be willing to stay in the race, ignore that loser clap, and go collect it.

Appendix:
My Community

TODAY I HAVE A NUMBER OF GOALS, but the primary one is to stay as healthy as possible for my family. Sheryl and I have many things we want to accomplish personally, the first of which is to continue traveling. The race has lit a fire in me for exploring the world; there are many places where I want to go and get lost in—deliberately this time. I also want to pursue being the best person I can be, living life to the fullest, meeting challenges head-on, and persevering when life gets tough.

Then, as I take care of me and mine, I want to turn my attention to those in the Parkinson's community and beyond. I hope to continue speaking for as long as possible, for as long as I've got something to say and an audience that finds it useful. There remains in me a strong desire to help heal the wounds that Parkinson's inflicts. To help educate where knowledge is lacking, to help strengthen bodies and limbs through physical activity, to help provide light, hope, and the will to persevere in even the darkest moments.

To live life well, we need to have a purpose. And for me, this has to be something that goes beyond just getting through the next day; it needs to be something that challenges me and does something for someone other than myself. I'm grateful not to be in this alone, and so I've delved into two avenues that I care passionately about.

One is advocacy work on behalf of people living with Parkinson's and their families. The other is child sponsorship with Compassion Canada. People understand the former, whereas the latter is met with an occasional raised eyebrow, an unspoken "How does that fit?" It fits because it has nothing to do with me. My work on behalf of children living in poverty reminds me that so many in our world are desperately poor; that no matter how bad my disease may get, I'll never be as bad off as they are.

In both my Parkinson's and my more general, corporate messages, I talk about physical fitness as an important component of what it means to Live Your Best. Dr. Becky Farley, a trained physical therapist at Parkinson Wellness Recovery (PWR), has spent years researching how physical activity positively impacts both the symptoms and the progression of Parkinson's disease. Our bodies appear to have been made to work best when we work them hard for an appropriate amount of time. Dr. Farley's impressive work should motivate us all to be more physically active.

It also provides daily inspiration and hope that, as individuals, there's something we can do to help control this disease. Having attended her PWR retreat, I've learned that you can revitalize both body and spirit through intense physical activity. Now, that retreat is not for the faint of heart; you learn very quickly that you're there to sweat. It's hard work, but the payoff is fantastic. The camaraderie, the joy of success, are life changing. Having some sense of control over a disease that otherwise feels all-consuming is a wonderful gift that Dr. Farley has given the Parkinson's community.

Why? Because I think we're sometimes out of balance in our earnest need to find a cure. Although I actively support the research, I'm skeptical that we'll see a cure in my lifetime. And so the bulk of my efforts are directed toward helping people maintain or improve their quality of life. We know with certainty that there are steps we can take now to help us live better with Parkinson's—making the day when a cure is discovered that much sweeter, since we'll be in that much better a position to enjoy its benefits.

I consider myself extraordinarily fortunate in having all the new friends and colleagues that Parkinson's has brought me. I'm continually learning from so many people around the world about how to live my best with the disease. From them I gain insight that in turn I can pass on to others.

It's been an incredible privilege to get to know Davis and Connie Carpenter Phinney of the Davis Phinney Foundation for Parkinson's. Along with their staff, I've seen their passion for bringing knowledge, inspiration, and hope to our Parkinson's tribe. Davis was diagnosed in his early forties after a successful cycling career. Along with his partner in life, Connie, he's built a foundation that many in the community look to for leadership in living with this disease.

I take great inspiration from these individuals, as well as the hundreds of unsung heroes I've met who daily battle this disease and show us what it means to Live Your Best. It's from their example that I find the strength and hope to move forward and offer what I can to the cause.

Giving speeches about my experiences in the race has opened doors into so many different lives like these. I've witnessed the fear and anxiety as well as the joy and achievement as others hear my story, find meaning in it, and choose to persevere. And each individual has a unique tale of perseverance that deserves to be heard.

Take Dan McGuire, for instance—an eighty-one-year-old from British Columbia who decided to ride his recumbent bike across Canada to raise awareness for the cause. Once he made it to Winnipeg, his daughter Tara called me and arranged for us to ride a few miles together. When I met him I was stunned. Here was this tottering, frail-looking old man (sorry, Dan!) who I couldn't imagine riding off the hotel parking lot, let alone across Canada. So much for my imagination—I'm quite sure Dan could still outride me to this day. He went on to complete his journey, once again proving that you can do more than you (or others) think. You just have to be willing to try. Dan's amazing story was chronicled online; you can see it at taramcguire.com/category/dads-journey.

Tim Jr. continues to be an inspiration for me, and many others, through the work he does on behalf of Parkinson's. To raise funds and awareness, he came up with the idea of a relay in which teams of five would compete to consume five hot wings and an eight-ounce glass of beer per team member (the event, as you may have guessed, is targeted at Tim Jr.'s age group). The fastest team takes home the championship, although the grand prize goes to the team that raises the most funds for Parkinson's. Tim Jr. has now held two separate events in Winnipeg and Fredericton, with up to twenty teams competing. To date, he's raised over thirty thousand dollars. I'm so proud of what he's accomplished, and look forward to all that he dreams of doing in the future for the cause. It's heartwarming to see his concern and compassion for me and others living with Parkinson's. You can follow his work at www.timjr.ca.

Now, through U-Turn Parkinson's, our family is attempting to help others live their best. We offer exercise classes that help mitigate the symptoms of Parkinson's, and for those dealing with the emotional pain this disease can bring, we offer friendship and support. We want to provide a voice for the community and a place of hope, not only to those with Parkinson's but also the family and friends who walk this journey with them.

Our focus is on wellness. I love how the National Wellness Institute in Wisconsin defines the term: "Wellness is an active process through which people become aware of, and make choices toward, a more successful existence." We want to offer a holistic approach to helping the community defeat this disease by looking at six core dimensions of wellness: physical, occupational, intellectual, spiritual, social, and emotional. If you're as fascinated with patterns as my good friend Daniel Friesen is, you may have noticed that these six dimensions almost perfectly spell the word "poise." That's a great word; it makes me think of things like grace, balance, control, steadiness—things that we in the Parkinson's community are working toward. So now we use the acronym POIS²E to help us remember the core dimensions we're helping to develop.

U-Turn just launched in 2016, and the board is considering what our next significant steps will be. We've already been involved with the Rock Steady Boxing program—a nonprofit organization that has made great strides in improving the physical fitness of those living with Parkinson's (and it's a lot of fun, too). Our hope is to soon move to other initiatives that will encourage people with Parkinson's to engage in more physical activity, such as yoga and cycling. That would cover the physical dimension; from there we'll branch out into the other five dimensions of wellness, engaging people with Parkinson's, their care partners, and the community at large.

One of our first areas of focus will be to support people when they're newly diagnosed—a time when, generally speaking, there are no straightforward means of getting resources into their hands. That's a woeful situation, one that leads to unnecessary stress and fear. We want to help people understand the disease and how it may affect their lives. Specifically, we want to establish a buddy system or mentorship—someone who understands and can walk alongside them in their new journey.

U-Turn wasn't established with a hefty endowment; it was funded by those who care about the cause. If you'd like to join them and help us, donations can be made at UTurnParkinsons.org. Of course, not everyone is in a position to make donations. I would encourage you to get involved with your local Parkinson's group. Join a walk, or host a support group and learn more about the disease— one that touches many lives, young and old alike. Many individuals tend to quietly bear the burden alone, not knowing that a community is there to help.

Of course, for me this journey is very personal. Having passed my sixth anniversary with Parkinson's, it remains my goal to be as healthy as possible for as long as possible for my family. I know the same is true for everyone else in the community. So the help you offer, whatever help that is, comes with my sincerest, heartfelt gratitude.

Acknowledgments

My heartfelt thanks goes out to these special people.

Rafa, if you had not come into our lives when you did then none of this may have ever happened. Thank you not only for setting it all in motion, but also for being such a wonderful addition to our family. Sheryl, you bring such beauty and adventure to our lives. I am forever grateful. Timothy, I am so proud to have run *The Amazing Race Canada* with you. You were the perfect partner and I know I could not have done it without you. Jordana, Eleni, Carter, and Kara, even though you did not run the race with us, I know that it has consumed much of your lives, too. Thank you for your patience and encouragement. Mom and Dad, Eleanor, what more can I say but thank you for all you've done for me.

To my book coach, Les Kletke, and my agent, Brian Wood, thank you for your expert guidance in getting me off the starting blocks. To my new friends at Penguin Random House Canada, thank you for this opportunity. Penguin Canada

Publisher, Nicole Winstanley, publicity expert Frances Bedford, marketing whiz Kara Carnduff, and my brilliant editor, Justin Stoller—it has been a wonderful experience working with each of you. Thank you for all the work that has gone in to bringing this project to completion.

To all those living with Parkinson's, thank you for the inspiration you continually provide me. And, finally, to the one who comes both first and last, the one who deserves all of my thanks, my God, Jesus Christ.

Index